BE
INFLUENTIAL

Surefire Ways to Improve
Your Presentation Skills

WHAT PEOPLE ARE SAYING

"I love good storytelling . . . and Shannon Alter is a very good storyteller. Shannon enhances this book with her passion, experience, empathy, and candor . . . and by painting a picture for the reader by drawing on her own personal stories; she invites us to 'try on' the concepts she is teaching, making them all the more relatable and immediately valuable. I was easily able to connect the concepts and stories with situations I have experienced in my life. I only wish Shannon had written this book 30 years ago!"

> – Barry Blanton, CPM®, Chief Problem Solver,
> Principal, Blanton Turner

"While reading Shannon's book I felt like I was sitting across a small table from her while she was giving me one-on-one advice on how to be successful in every imaginable speaking opportunity. This book is filled with great stories and tips for both the beginner speaker and the pro."

> – Richard Muhlebach, CPM®, CRE®, RPA®, SCSM®, CRX®,
> Vice President, Bond Retail

"The most innovative ideas come from a medley of distinct experiences, and Shannon Alter proves just that. Using lessons learned as a leading commercial real estate pro, further enhanced by her theatrical background, she provides easy-to-read tips and tricks when developing and presenting to an audience.

How wonderful would it have been to have had a guide like this when I first started my career! Shannon provides conversational coaching skills with great humor, excellent examples, videos, and exercises. This is a must-read for anyone who presents to one person or fifty, whether at their desk or on stage."

> – Becky Hanner, CPM®, RPA®, LEED Green Associate,
> Principal, Commercial Asset Services & Crestmark
> Commercial

WHAT PEOPLE ARE SAYING

"I would highly recommend the book *Be Influential* by Shannon Alter. It is an excellent resource for anyone looking to improve their communication skills—from everyday conversations to high-stakes situations. This book provides real-world examples and tips for how to navigate uncertainty, manage emotions, and build trust—truly demonstrating influence in action. It's easy to read, digest, and put ideas into quick action. I can't wait to share this with my colleagues and friends!"

> – Denise LeDuc Froemming, CPA, CAE®,
> President & CEO at California Society of CPAs

"I enjoyed the easy and insightful read of this new book on speaking! Having presented hundreds/thousands of times, for meetings, conferences, and events, this is a great go-to book on focusing your message, reading the audience, and making great eye contact while connecting with your listeners. I would highly recommend this DIY book for those starting their speaking careers, elevating their careers, or for experienced speakers who need a refresher."

> – John K. Scott, RPA®, BOMA Fellow, Regional Managing
> Director, Southeast and Mid-Central Regions,
> Real Estate Management and Services, Colliers

"Shannon really covered it all in *Be Influential*. This book is full of great in-depth functional knowledge, stories, and practical solutions everyone can use, whether they are newer professionals or experienced ones. I enjoyed reading this book and recommend having your highlighter in hand to mark up all of the great resources you'll want to use!"

> – Bob Osbrink, EVP, Market Leader,
> Matthews Real Estate Investment Services

BE
INFLUENTIAL

Surefire Ways to Improve Your Presentation Skills

Shannon Alter

Leaders Exceed, LLC

Be Influential: Surefire Ways to Improve Your Presentation Skills
Published by Leaders Exceed, LLC
Santa Ana, California, U.S.A.

ALTER, SHANNON, Author
BE INFLUENTIAL
SHANNON ALTER

Library of Congress Control Number: 2023905796

ISBN: 979-8-218-14552-1, 979-8-9882081-1-2 (paperback)
ISBN: 979-8-9882081-0-5 (hardcover)
ISBN: 979-8218-16824-7 (digital)

BUSINESS & ECONOMICS / Business Communication / Meetings & Presentations
SELF-HELP / Communication & Social Skills

Editing & Design: Nadia Geagea Pupa (piquepublishing.com)
Publishing Management: Susie Schaefer (finishthebookpublishing.com)
Public Relations: Laura Perkes (prwithperkes.com)

QUANTITY PURCHASES: Schools, companies, professional groups, clubs, and other organizations may qualify for special terms when ordering quantities of this title. For information, email Shannon@LeadersExceed.com.

TO JEFF, HAYLEY, AND SARAH,
THANK YOU FOR BEING THE LIGHTS OF MY LIFE

CONTENTS

WELCOME VIDEO

My name is Shannon Alter and I am pleased that you have taken the first steps towards improving your presentation skills.

The book contains a number of tools, tips, and exercises that you will be able to use, everyday.

SCAN THIS QR CODE
TO WATCH MY
WELCOME VIDEO.

INTRODUCTION

NOT LONG AGO, I WAS CHATTING WITH A COLLEAGUE ABOUT AN important presentation she'd recently given. When I asked how it went, she said, "I confess. I was reading my notes." I asked why, and she hesitated for a moment, then said, "I thought there were only going to be two other people in the meeting, but when I walked in, there were actually ten. I just kind of panicked and my brain froze! I didn't know what else to do to get through the presentation."

If you've experienced this same feeling of dread, you're probably wondering how you can solve this problem. Here's the good news: it's easier than you think.

WHAT'S YOUR PRESENTATION NIGHTMARE?

Do you have recurring nightmares a few days before you're about to give an important talk? If you're like me, it happens like clockwork. When I first started speaking and training, I would have stress dreams, especially the night before. Usually, my nightmare went something like this: I'd arrived at the venue for my presentation, only to find that the door was locked, it was the wrong day, or I had massive bed head while wearing the wrong clothes. I'd even dream that I was onstage and dropped a stack of notes that scattered everywhere, and worst of all, I'd completely forgotten what to say.

Those vivid, distressful dreams never came true, but they did illustrate my secret panic as a novice presenter! My presentation nightmares caused my worry to overflow. Fortunately, I knew there must be a knack for improving my presentation skills.

HOW CAN THIS BOOK HELP YOU?

Throughout this book, you'll discover tactics you can successfully use in any conversation, long or short, formal or informal. Consider these five scenarios:

- You're included in a sales pitch, but you aren't the salesperson
- You're meeting with your boss or your leadership team
- You're presenting at a board meeting
- You're meeting with your child's coach or teacher
- You're not the leader or person of authority in the meeting

Imagine the many interactions, personal and professional, we have with others every day. Despite our best efforts, they don't always flow smoothly! You might even feel embarrassed by the way you responded, especially if you were caught off guard.

Even if you don't pitch proposals every day, you'll find that this book will help you every time you're preparing for a conversation or presentation. My goal is to help you zero in on surefire, consistent ways to improve the way you present yourself and communicate with others. You can apply the tactics you'll discover in this book to successfully navigate not only these situations but any conversation, long or short, formal or informal.

But first, you must pinpoint the problems.

Imagine you're about to give a presentation tomorrow. Ask yourself these questions:

- Do you feel prepared?
- Is your presentation organized?
- Do you have a presentation routine?
- Do you feel confident handling questions?

When I think back on what I did to improve my own presentation skills, I discovered something huge: my clients, colleagues, and friends felt the same way I did! They were uncertain about how to start, what to say, and how to display confidence, poise, and expertise.

Recently, a colleague called me, pleading for help. He asked if I could sit in on a meeting—that same afternoon! His team was preparing to pitch the management of an important real estate property to a new, highly visible prospective client. If they aced the meeting, more new accounts could follow. The problem was that he had to leave town suddenly due to an emergency, meaning he couldn't sit in on the pitch.

"My A-team is lined up and ready to go," he said. "I know I can trust you to give me your honest opinion on the meeting. They've done this a lot, so it should be routine for them." As I hustled over to the meeting room, I wondered, *Did they actually rehearse the pitch?* Well, not exactly.

This potential client was well-known for requiring a lot of attention to detail. Before handshakes were even out of the way, the president (and potential client) looked my colleague's manager right in the eye and asked, "So, John, what did you notice on your visit to our property?"

John was clearly taken by surprise. "Uh," he blurted, "I actually haven't seen the property yet." Oops! In that moment, you could have heard a pin drop! As you might guess, the silence was indeed awkward, and it took some time for the rest of the team to recover the conversation.

Unwittingly, John had broken an important rule: preparation pays off. He was so focused on setting up his presentation slides that he hadn't considered how to handle a question he couldn't answer, and his team didn't have a Plan B. It happens to all of us! When I first started out, I often felt pressed for time or thought my team had already held so many similar conversations that we knew it cold and didn't need to rehearse.

Whether you're honing new skills or refining existing ones, this book will help you polish your presentations and make your meetings and conversations shine. We'll uncover the things that trip you up and how you can overcome them. Perhaps you need help developing your confidence and executive presence. Or you may not understand how to set the tone or know what to include (and what to leave out). Maybe you're an expert at what you do, but you struggle to convey your message clearly, or to find the stories that will best connect with your audience. You might even struggle with wanting to appear spontaneous and often end up "winging it."

Throughout this book, I share sample scenarios and give you tools and exercises that you can use immediately, both personally and professionally. Some of these tools and exercises include:

- Five questions to ask when editing your presentation

- Learning how to "read the room"
- Tactics you can use to frame your message
- Using a self-video to quell the jitters
- Walking through a presentation checklist (aka pregame checklist)
- Strategies to handle questions

And here's the best part: These solutions work for almost any conversation or presentation. They'll help you when making a business case to your boss, presenting an idea to your team, guiding an employee, or collaborating with another department.

P.S. If you're wondering what happened to my nightmares, once I focused on using the tools and exercises outlined in this book, those horrible nightmares waned. Some of my jitters remain, but a tiny bit of stage fright can keep you on your toes.

EXAMINE YOUR FEARS OF PUBLIC SPEAKING

There you are, at the front of a room, leading your team meeting. Unexpectedly, your boss walks in. Suddenly, a trickle of sweat makes its way down your back. Your palms are clammy, and you have a tickle in your throat. You feel a little dizzy. If this has happened to you, you're not alone. There's a name for it: *glossophobia*. According to Healthline, glossophobia happens when we feel uncertain or afraid and our body has a natural fight-or-flight response. There's good news, though. Glossophobia can usually be resolved, and this book can help you do it.

Those of us who aren't involved in public speaking know firsthand that fear—or plain old stage fright—*can* get the better of you. It's estimated that four out of ten Americans are afraid of speaking in public. Experts tell us that many people fear public speaking more than anything else. In fact, comedian Jerry Seinfeld joked, "This means, to the average person, if you have to be at a funeral, you would rather be in the casket than doing the eulogy."

At a conference, I asked the audience what they *didn't* enjoy about public speaking; a hand immediately shot up. "There's really nothing about it I like! Everyone is looking at me, and I wind up feeling awkward." Another colleague chimed in: "I agree. If I can talk with you one on one, I'm great. But when I have to get up in front of any size group, my confidence flies out the window." A third hand flew up. "I'm okay if I have a script," a woman said, "but if anything throws me off, I'm toast." Here we were, in a big group, and these people were bonding over their shared fears of presenting in front of exactly that—a big group!

Often, we're stuck in our own heads—me included. A few years ago, I decided to take an acting class. I speak and train for a living, so I figured it would be a piece of cake. I signed up for an advanced acting class with a regional theater in my area. When I arrived for the first night of class, my first thought was, *What on earth have I done? These people are professional actors and I am not!*

Our instructor designed the class to include scenes from Shakespeare and Chekhov. I tend to be more of a modern girl, and if you've ever read these great playwrights, you know that by today's standards, the language can be difficult. Especially if you're stuck in your own head. I discovered a great lesson: I had to learn to listen—*really* listen—to the other actor in my scene. If I was not listening, or thinking of my grocery list or work to-dos, the scene wouldn't work, and what I did (or didn't) do would affect the other actors. Getting out of your head is key.

Executives, managers, and students alike often describe common anxieties when required to speak in front of almost anybody.

On a scale of 1 (lowest) to 5 (highest), how would you score yourself on the following six statements?

Personal Assessment on Presentation Skills

I don't like getting up in front of people.

1	2	3	4	5

I talk too fast and almost always finish early.

1	2	3	4	5

People cannot hear me.

1	2	3	4	5

I forget what I am saying.

1	2	3	4	5

Nerves get the better of me.

1	2	3	4	5

I don't know where to look.

1	2	3	4	5

If you scored 20 or higher, don't worry. For many of us, the mere thought of public speaking evokes a fight-or-flight response. We start to feel like Dorothy in *The Wizard of Oz*: we'd rather be home.

DO YOU WANT TO BE INFLUENTIAL IN YOUR INDUSTRY?

Take baby steps. Here's your first exercise:

What successful presentations or meetings have you attended, whether in person or virtual, and **why** *do you think they were successful?*

It doesn't matter whether you participated as a speaker, an audience member, or a meeting attendee. What matters is identifying specific things that made the presentation a success. Think deeply about these questions—reflect not just on *what*, but on *why*:

- Did the presentation flow smoothly?
- Did the presenter seem relaxed and poised?
- Did the presenter have presence?
- Did the speaker's tone feel conversational?
- Was the presentation engaging?
- If the presenter used slides, did they add value?
- Was the overall setting pleasant?

Now, here's the most important part of this exercise: After you finish this book, revisit these questions and do the exercise again. Then, compare your answers. I promise, it'll be an eye-opening experience!

PRACTICE, POISE, AND POLISH: THE KEY TO GREAT PRESENTATIONS

Even those of us who enjoy speaking in front of people regularly encounter a few glitches along the way. Take a moment and think about a few public speakers you admire. These speakers might hold celebrity status or be high-profile executives. Or they could be a coworker, your boss, a client, or a teacher. Ask yourself, what makes them so well-spoken?

Excellent speakers consistently maintain certain stellar traits. They are:

- Confident
- Charismatic
- Calm
- Poised
- Informative
- Entertaining
- Influential

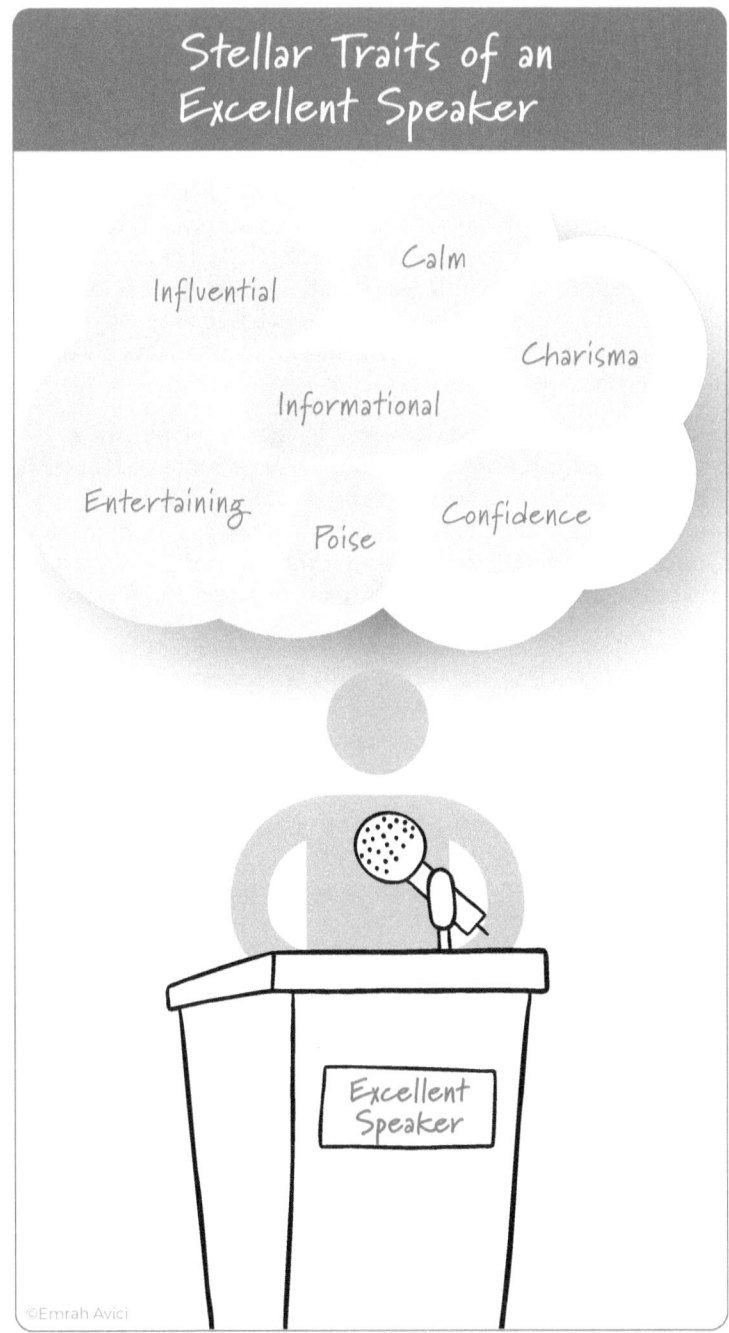

Always remember that you also have the power to develop these same traits.

I had a client who was recently promoted to an executive role at a large corporate office. He wasn't sure what he needed to do to improve his presentation skills. "I don't give presentations every day, and I'm not in sales," he explained. His main challenge was leading client and employee meetings. He lacked confidence and would get really, *really* nervous. This showed up when he spoke: His voice shook, he rambled, and he was, well, a little bit fidgety. He was unable to deliver his message clearly and succinctly and always left feeling dissatisfied. So did his teams and clients, because they would always follow up with additional questions and concerns.

There always seemed to be a disconnect. He was unable to communicate clearly and succinctly and always left feeling dissatisfied. So did his teams and clients, because they would always follow up with additional questions and concerns. Although he was a capable leader—after all, he'd done something right to get the promotion in the first place—there was a disconnect between his message and his delivery.

Here's how we helped him solve these issues: We worked together for several months on honing and refining his skills, whether in person or virtually. We discovered that he had many impressive strengths, but there were specific things that blocked him when it came time to present information to groups of executives—both large and small.

We conducted various exercises, had many casual conversations, and found ways to increase his confidence and help him present more smoothly and sound more polished in any professional conversation he had. Afterward, his boss gave me a call: "I noticed that he's organized in a way he never was before. Now he has a Plan B if things go awry. He's also more poised and relaxed and is able to answer questions. Having you coach him on his presentation and communication skills has made a big difference in his job performance."

In this book, I share the in-depth exercises, tools, tips, and methods that I use with all of my clients. Each time, they walk away feeling much more confident in themselves as speakers, presenters, and experts in their industries. Think of this book as your own personal-guided tour and coaching plan. I provide examples, stories, and tactics you can use to not only improve your own speaking skills but, most importantly, become more influential.

Throughout the book, look for QR codes that lead to my videos. And because practice is key to your success, I've included short exercises to complete at the end of every chapter. These activities are the best tools you can use when you're preparing for a conversation with a peer, presenting to your team or client, or demonstrating a business case. I hope you will implement them!

I'LL SEE YOU AT THE FINISH LINE

Whatever your goals are, you can transform into a calm, confident, relaxed, and influential speaker in front of any audience. Whether you are a business leader, association executive, college student, or young professional, this book will teach you surefire ways to quell your nerves, effectively target your audience, and clearly convey your message in any meeting or conversation.

By implementing my tools, techniques, and tips, you'll gain the skills you need to deliver solid, successful presentations and get rave reviews—each and every time.

CHAPTER 1
LET'S GET STARTED!

WHEN I FIRST STARTED SPEAKING AND FACILITATING, I wrote *everything* down—literally every single thing—on a long yellow legal pad. This, I figured, was my road to confidence! Even though I was a novice speaker, I reasoned this would be the easiest way to capture every last bit of the information I wanted to convey! After all, I could just zone in to the parts I wanted when I needed to refer to a note, right? I was wrong on all counts.

Like many of us, I wasn't sure exactly how to effectively use the pages and pages of notes I had so laboriously written out. I'm a girl with a plan, however, and I had a Plan B: *this* would save the day!

It took just a few minutes for me to realize that the technique I had devised was far from a slam dunk. While flexibility is definitely a strength, tactic number two also bombed. Here's what actually happened: I pulled out a pile of 3" × 5" index cards I'd brought with me, just in case. You know, the kind with the lines—you may have once used them in school or the library (or at least heard of them). I'd managed to cram in a few points on each one. But as luck would have it, I dropped them all, right in front of my audience! It was remarkably like the old game of pick-up sticks you may have played as a kid. What did I do? I decided quickly that the best course of action was to chuckle, pick up the cards, and keep on going. My audience chuckled along with me, which in turn put everyone at ease.

Right then, I decided that experiencing so many blunders in just one public speaking session had to have a silver lining—and it did. That's where this book comes in! My goal is to help *you* by sharing what didn't work for me, how I changed what I was doing to become successful, and how you can benefit.

This book provides you with a surefire, practical method to use for any presentation or conversation. I've done a lot of research and will share those ideas with you throughout this book. Whether you're delivering a pitch, presenting a business case to your boss, preparing for a team meeting, or having a conversation with your child's sports coach, you'll discover tactics that really work and a rinse-and-repeat process you can use successfully, every time.

I've included exercises at the end of each chapter. When I work with clients, we use these exercises (and more) throughout our workshops so participants can see how applying them will immediately change their own approach to presentations—for the better. Tip: Try these exercises the next time you have a team or leadership meeting back in your office (either your virtual or hybrid office). You'll get instant engagement and conversation, and you'll be able to zero in on what your team really needs. Who could ask for more?

WHAT TRIPS YOU UP WHEN YOU'RE PRESENTING?

When I meet with executive leaders or present at a conference, I always ask this question: "What trips you up when you're presenting and where do you feel less than confident?" Not surprisingly, the responses are fast and furious. "FEAR!" shouted one participant at a recent meeting. "I just know whatever I've planned to say isn't coming out of my mouth the way I want it to."

Another attendee quickly tagged on: "Vulnerability—giving away too much information." "Being concise," added a third person. "I always feel I'm taking too long and then I start to stumble."

Imagine you're about to start an important client presentation, speaking at an employee meeting, or delivering a talk to one hundred of your closest colleagues. The outcome of this presentation is critical, and you are . . . well, more than a little bit nervous. You're new in your role, and you haven't even met all the participants yet. You're positive everyone is judging your abilities.

Quickly, you scan the room; there are only two people you know. Your heart plummets. As you head to the front, you realize everyone is looking right at—you. To make matters even worse, only a short squeak comes out of your mouth, and you're starting to sweat. Panicking, your mind races to remember your speech but it's . . . blank. You're pretty sure you're done, right then and there. What can you do?

The secret is this: blunders can happen anywhere! On the day of my legal pad snafu, I'd tried to carefully curate my outfit in advance. After I'd cleaned up the scattered index cards, a participant in the front row whispered to me: "Shannon, did you know you have two different earrings on?" Indeed I did; I was wearing a small stud in one ear and a big, chunky hoop in the other. My daughter was only a few months old and getting dressed successfully took a little time—I was lucky both my shoes matched! Did that ratchet my nerves up to a 10? You bet!

Now, let's go back to the scenario I described at the beginning of this chapter. In fact, there were more than a few obstacles blocking my path to success. My list may look familiar to you:

- The long, thick legal pad I had brought along was cumbersome and had pages and pages of bullet points and scribbles. While using bullet points was good, including absolutely everything because I was afraid of missing something was not so good.
- My eyesight is great, but deciphering my handwritten notes while talking and interacting wasn't. Since I was looking down at my notes the whole time, my connection with the audience faded from the get-go. If there's a choice, it's much better to look up and connect with your audience than to be 100 percent word-perfect.
- There was no way I'd be able to find the right "reminder" in time to finish the talk! I wound up focusing more on searching my notes than actually having a conversation. Tip: It's fine to write your script out at first. The trick is to then throw it out!

START HERE

The skills and techniques you'll learn in this book will prepare you for the multiple interactions you have every day (even if they involve wardrobe malfunctions). Begin with these steps:

Decide on Your Topic

A colleague mentioned recently that an association she belonged to had asked her to speak at one of their meetings. She was excited and honored, but she realized they didn't assign her a specific topic. Instead, they asked for her ideas. "Well," she said, "I can talk about a lot of things. How do I do that?" The key here is to first listen to what your client tells you they need and want. Then you can continue discussing what the options are. If you offer to include everything, you'll often wind up including almost nothing.

For example, I probably *can* talk about time management, but I don't. It isn't in my wheelhouse and would just be me offering my opinion. If someone asked me for that topic, I'd refer them to another exceptional speaker and let them know how I can share another topic that is in my area of expertise: communications.

This is important, because once you actually decide what your topic is, it makes everything easier. Throughout this book, I'll describe how to stay on track once you do decide.

Do Your Research

Imagine how you'd feel if you could nail every presentation, every time. Awesome, right? Taking the time to do your homework in advance can make all the difference, no matter what your topic is. Here are three ways you can zero in with just a little research. Psst . . . stay tuned for Chapter 3, which is all about how to organize and map out your presentation or conversation.

■ **Start with a Presentation SWOT Analysis**

Now that you know what stumps you and what issues can trip you up when you're about to have an important conversation or give a presentation, it's time to take the next step: do a SWOT (Strengths, Weaknesses, Opportunities, Threats) analysis. I recommend this exercise because it's such a helpful tool to show you where you are and where you want to be. In fact, I use a similar tool with my executive coaching clients. We do it twice: once right at the start of our coaching sessions and once again at our windup.

You may already be familiar with this tool, or even use a similar one in your business. For example, if you're in the real estate field, perhaps you've used this tool to analyze buildings or properties. Almost any business can use it to better gauge the areas where they want to focus.

I've included a sample worksheet to use as you go through this exercise. You can pull this out now to follow along. There are four quadrants: S (Strengths), W (Weaknesses), O (Opportunities), and T (Threats). Use each quadrant to help evaluate your (or your organization's) ability to present and convey your message.

For example, if you're filling in the "Strengths" quadrant, your responses could be:

- I'm very conversational.
- I look confident even when I'm nervous.
- My team has several experienced speakers.

When you're looking at "Weaknesses," perhaps you'll note:

- My team is good at talking, but we're not always great at listening.
- I feel my body language makes me look like I'm not poised or confident.
- It's hard to get my team to practice together so we appear cohesive.

Under "Opportunities," you could list opportunities that might present themselves:

- I can be a "fly on the wall" in another meeting.
- I have a more experienced colleague who can serve as a model.
- My team can try to rehearse more.

In the "Threats" quadrant, you could note what might keep you from presenting smoothly:

- Someone else on the team tends to take over.
- I'm not the leader in the meeting.
- I don't know my child's teacher or coach very well.
- My body language doesn't match my words.

Keep this sample exercise on hand—it's a great way to tell your story!

SWOT Analysis	
Strengths	Weaknesses
Opportunities	Threats

■ **Ask Questions**

That's right, just ask. There's no better way to gather intel about a leadership team, for example. If I'm doing a presentation for an employee department or division, I often ask the leader I'm working with how I can hear in advance from other leaders on the team. I've done this by scheduling brief phone interviews, joining in on their leadership meeting, or even surveying their employees or association members.

When I survey or ask questions, I make it short, four to five questions at most. My goal is to hear what *they* have to say.

■ **Think about How You'll Field Questions**

Think about how you'll answer questions. We'll describe this in more detail later, but I want you to keep in mind how this can work for you as you read this book.

While I was writing this chapter, my colleague Janelle called to say she was planning a small group training class, and she was a little nervous. When I asked what she felt the issue was, she replied, "I'm worried about how to handle questions. I just want to give them the best answers."

Not wanting to be stumped by a spontaneous query on her somewhat technical topic, she decided to have small cards or paper available so her attendees could write down their questions during the presentation, which would then be passed up to her. This was a great idea: it allowed her audience to think about their questions, and it allowed her a moment to digest them before responding.

Best of all, the relief she felt was palpable. "My shoulders just relaxed immediately," she said. "I was able to spend my time thinking about the actual questions rather than about how I was going to handle them. Whew!"

Of course, when I work with executive leaders, there are many different activities and exercises we choose from, as described later in this book.

Use These Two Winning Tactics

1. Edit, edit, edit! Determine what your audience wants to know and give it to them! Don't make them wait—and wade through your entire presentation—to find out what your point is. Of course, you do need to know all the background information for your conversation, but you don't need to include it all in the conversation—that's a surefire way to lose your listeners.

2. Have a Plan A. Have a Plan B. And a Plan C. And perhaps even a Plan D. Whether you're presenting virtually or in person, stuff happens. For example, another way to handle questions is to have a few "seed" questions tucked in your back pocket. They're a useful way to anticipate what the questions will be before they are even asked.

Concisely editing what you're going to say and having a no-fail backup plan (or plans) are critical.

— CHAPTER 1 EXERCISE —

Here's how to start: First, think about what you can do in just five minutes. This brainstorming exercise will take only five minutes but will help you clarify what works for you and where you may want to improve.

1. Think about what trips *you* up most when you have an upcoming presentation or important conversation.

2. Grab a sheet of paper, a Post-it, or your phone, and quickly jot down five to seven things that are obstacles for you to a successful presentation. Don't deliberate, write long notes, or revise. A simple jot does the trick.

To spark some ideas, revisit the questions below, which I shared in the introduction. Be sure to save your notes so you can compare later when you're at the end of the book.

· Do you feel prepared?
· Is your presentation organized?
· Do you have a presentation routine?
· Do you feel confident handling questions?

3. Now, circle the *three* things that concern you the most or you've received the most feedback on. You might be thinking, *I have at least ten things that are bothering me!* While this could be true, there's a reason for circling three items only. It can be hard to incorporate solutions to ten different areas right away. Whittling down your list to three will help you focus and see quicker results. Post your list within eyesight right now so it will be top of mind as you work through this book.

CHAPTER 2
SETTING THE FOUNDATION:
ROCK SOLID

B RAD, A COLLEAGUE WHO WAS PREPARING FOR HIS FIRST BIG presentation, called me recently for advice on his topic. He'd been invited to speak at his company's leadership meeting. "I confess," he said, "I don't know exactly what to talk about. I'm a bit all over the place." When I asked about the meeting format, he replied, "I was too afraid to ask! I want to impress my boss, and I feel like I should know this already."

"You've got this!" I said. "This happens all the time." Here's the truth: almost everyone has struggled at some point with making a presentation or having a critical conversation, whether in their career or just in life. But if you take the time to set the foundation for your talk in advance—whatever the subject—you'll absolutely feel more confident. Added bonus: your shoulders will immediately relax too!

The strategy I outline here really does work, each and every time. What's the kicker? You, my friend, will have to be diligent. If by nature you're more inclined to wing it, this approach may be different than what you're used to. But there's a method to my madness. Once you get the process down, I promise you, you'll be comfortable and poised in any presentation.

Hint: You can easily use this right back in your own office (or your virtual office).

In this chapter, you'll learn how to set this all-important foundation. We'll home in on how to:

- Determine the type of presentation you'll deliver
- Decide on your topic
- Figure out the format
- Use a pregame checklist
- Establish your purpose

DETERMINE THE TYPE OF PRESENTATION

First, think about the typical types of conversations or presentations you might be involved in, depending on your role. Of course, there are many other factors to consider, such as timing, content, and audience. I'll explain those later on.

Meeting with your boss and/or company leadership: In my experience, this is one of the most common types of presentations we're likely to give at work. Like Brad, my colleague who was prepping for his first big presentation, you may be preparing for a special conversation with your boss or presenting performance results to your leadership team. This could also be an internal department or division meeting where you're doing training or asked to take the lead on a topic.

Pitch for a potential client: In the introduction, I described a pitch-gone-wrong situation with an unprepared team. Occasionally, we can successfully "wing it." Often, we feel that if we aren't in sales, we don't need to worry about getting our pitch right, or we feel we're not really "pitching." The fact is, whether or not you're actually in sales, you're selling all the time: to clients, to peers, to your boss. Think about it—we're often trying to persuade someone else to do what we need them to do, regardless of whether it's actually a sales call.

Keynote: Keynote presentations generally open or close a meeting or conference and are often motivational and centered around the meeting's theme. Traditionally, keynoters directly address the audience; however, there is usually not much interaction. There can be many variations on this: celebrity oriented, entertainment, etc.

Workshop or breakout meeting: A workshop or a breakout meeting is typically offered on a specific topic (it can be tactical or leadership oriented), is interactive, and can be done internally at an organization or at an outside meeting (e.g., for an association, an internal leadership meeting, or a conference). Often this is also defined by timing. For example, I may do a half- or full-day highly interactive workshop for a client, or an hour-long session for an association. Breakout sessions can also offer a deeper dive around a central theme.

A key element here is to remember that our audience wants to leave with takeaways they can use. They want to be armed with foundational knowledge on your topic, plus action items and resources they can explore afterward. When you're preparing for your talk, you can easily sketch out those takeaways by highlighting them or making a quick note to yourself. If you feel you may forget them, jot a few one-word bullets on a Post-it note as a reminder.

Panel: Many of us have likely seen or even participated in a panel discussion. You'll see this format at internal company leadership meetings, association meetings, and conferences, largely because it's an efficient way to include several experts to discuss a specific topic. These are typically moderated, or one panelist acts as the moderator to keep the conversation flowing.

DECIDE ON YOUR TOPIC

Think about it this way: every "presentation" or program is actually just a conversation, and one of your most important steps is just to *decide*. That's right, no matter who your audience is, you have to settle on your topic and stick with it.

Brad's story is a great example: When we met in person, he brought along an entire backpack full to the brim with notes and books. His topic? Market trends for his industry. Period. That's a huge subject, and he was likely to lose his audience if he kept it that way.

The good news was that Brad had loads of industry knowledge and credibility. He just didn't know how to narrow down his topic. He wanted to include everything he could (and everything he knew) so his audience (his leadership team) wouldn't miss anything. What he really needed was to whittle it down so he could be sure his points would stick with his audience.

Try This Simple Hack!
Grab your nearest pack of Post-its and try this simple four-step process to help you decide. You can do it on a whiteboard, or on your desk or even a wall—any flat surface will do.

Step 1: Write each of your ideas for your main topic on a separate Post-it and stick it up on the board. It doesn't matter how many there are, and they don't need to be in any specific order.

Step 2: Do the same with any subtopics you have in mind. Get them up on the board too.

Step 3: Now, choose your three top topics, the ones you like best and feel are most relevant. Consider whether a topic is too broad, too light, or better suited for another talk. Place these at the top of the board and do the same with the subtopics. Don't throw out the remaining Post-it topics yet. Just put them on one side of your board or down at the bottom—they're in reserve.

Step 4: This is the hard part: pick one topic only—yep, only one—and three subtopics, just in case. This will be a great starting point! As for the "reserve" topics you've put to the side, keep them—they may come in handy.

When I do executive and presentation skills coaching, settling on a topic is one of the first areas we focus on. I'll share more tips for exactly how to edit your own talk as we go through this book.

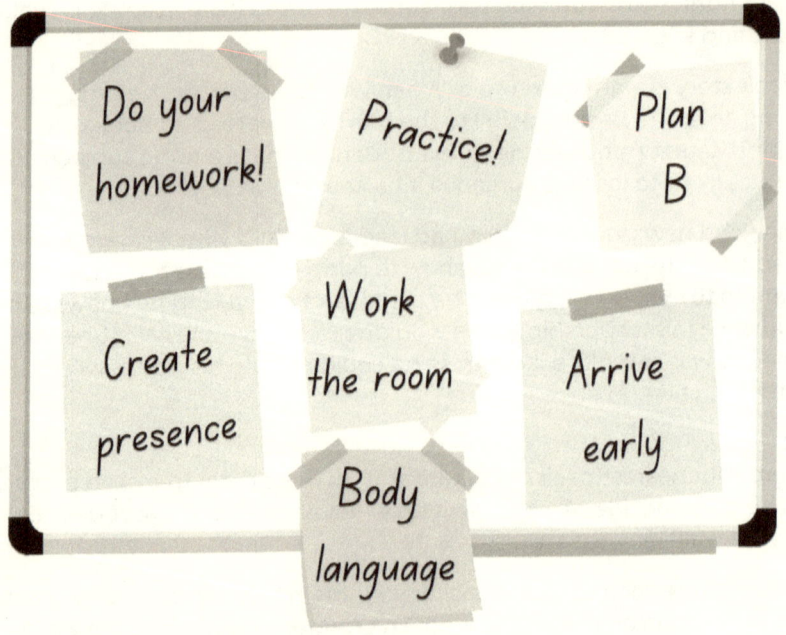

FIGURE OUT THE FORMAT

When we have the opportunity to speak in front of a group or lead a meeting, we're often so excited about it that we don't always think about where we're going to be—literally. I'll describe this more in later chapters; however, I include it here because understanding where you'll be will help you map out your plan.

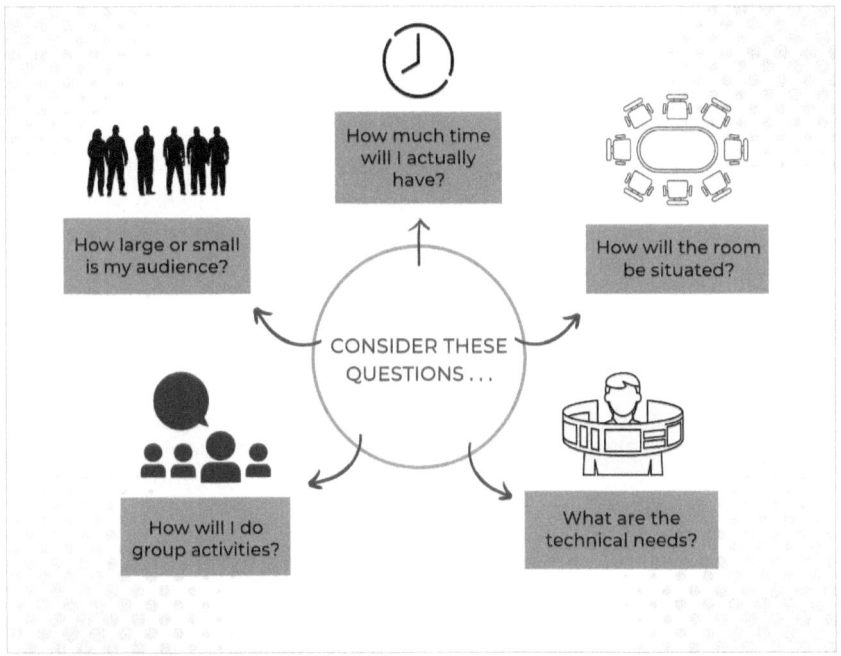

ESTABLISH YOUR PURPOSE

Here's where the strategy comes in. Why are you up on stage in the first place, and why does your topic matter? Typically, your talk will fall into one of these categories:

My objective is to . . .

Analyze: Perhaps you're tasked with reviewing your department, division, or company sales or financial performance in front of your CFO or leadership team.

Inform: This is pretty straightforward and could include advising and informing your team of new policies or standard monthly reporting to a client.

Instruct: Training fits into this category. Instruction is where we teach and facilitate a certain topic for our team, our audience, or our students, with the goal of helping them become more proficient in that area.

Persuade: We persuade every day, whether it's making a business case to our boss, pitching a service or account to a prospective client, or convincing our audience to take action or our team and peers to make a change.

Motivate: Motivational talks are intended to inspire audience members to change their behavior in some way, make a decision, or implement a change.

The tone you set for your presentation will create interest and demonstrate passion, and that may just invite your audience to make a change, implement an action step, take a chance, or simply learn something new that will stick with them long after your presentation.

— CHAPTER 2 EXERCISE —

Try writing out the objective for your talk in a single sentence. This is similar to defining your organization's mission statement. Here are a few examples:

> **My goal is to educate employers on how to hire great employees.**

> **I want to persuade this prospective client that working with our firm is the best decision they will make.**

You get the idea. Keep this objective in mind as you prepare, and find a way to reinforce it throughout your talk. When you do this, your message will stick with your audience, and, better yet, you'll have more influence with them.

We're all busy and probably suffering from information overload—this is one place where repetition is a great thing!

CHAPTER 3
CONFIDENCE: OWNING THE ROOM

ARLY ON IN MY CAREER, MY FAVORITE MENTOR AND I WERE meeting over coffee one morning when he leaned in across the table. This was my first senior leadership role, and I needed some advice on getting my point across to the people who mattered most: our clients and our team.

"Here's the secret," he said. "*Every*body sells. And everyone makes an instant impression when they walk into a room. Make yours count."

It was all I could do not to sputter, "But I'm not in a sales role! I don't do pitches!"

Wiser than me, he countered, "Ah, but you're a leader. You communicate with your peers, your clients, and your team—all the time. Don't underestimate the value of learning what image you want to convey, right from the get-go. Believe me, you'll use this skill."

And he was right! He was talking about developing executive presence. I was lucky to work with this particular leader, although I didn't recognize it at the time.

We were in the hospitality business, each from different divisions. I was absolutely positive (and absolutely wrong) that he didn't—and couldn't—know anything from a technical standpoint about my team's side of the business.

Although he didn't know the day-to-day details, he knew hospitality, and more importantly, he excelled at leadership. Every morning, we sat together for just a few minutes to discuss plans for the day. I didn't realize it then, but what he was teaching me was how to have confidence. I admit it—in my eagerness to model him, I was just a little too bold. It took a while for me to learn from his approachability and figure out how to frame both my confidence and my presence.

Whether you're up at the front of the room giving a presentation or meeting one on one with a prospective client, your ability to "own the room"—to deliver both presence and impact—is key. It all comes down to how we communicate and present ourselves, even before we walk into a room.

Our nonverbal cues have a lot to do with what we believe about ourselves, in any conversation or presentation. Social psychologist Amy Cuddy popularized the concept of "power posing" in her 2012 TEDGlobal talk, "Your body language may shape who you are." Cuddy shows us how this evidence of confidence and presence makes all the difference.

Cuddy's conclusion resulted partly from a study she conducted to determine how powerful participants felt after sitting in either "high" or "low" power poses for two minutes. A high-power pose is expansive; a low-power pose appears inward. Power posing is simply a way to manage your body language to project confidence *and* to then feel more powerful. The idea is that if you stand in a posture you associate with power, you will feel powerful.

TRY THIS EXPERIMENT

The next time you have a leadership meeting, have your team view Cuddy's video in advance. This is a great opportunity to have your team experiment with low-power and high-power poses. First, break them into groups of two or three and ask them to choose a scenario where they are planning a presentation or conversation. Then, have them trade off practicing both types of power poses as preparation before they enter their intended meeting. This is a fun exercise to do that is sure to give your team added insight!

HOW YOU CAN OWN THE ROOM

What happens when you're in an important presentation and everything you planned to say flies right out the window? Of course, we've all had that feeling! When we're panicked, we naturally resort to whatever feels most comfortable. And whether you're meeting with your team, your boss, or a client, they all want to feel that you're confident, calm, and have everything under control. Cultivating and elevating your own executive presence will help you polish your presentations.

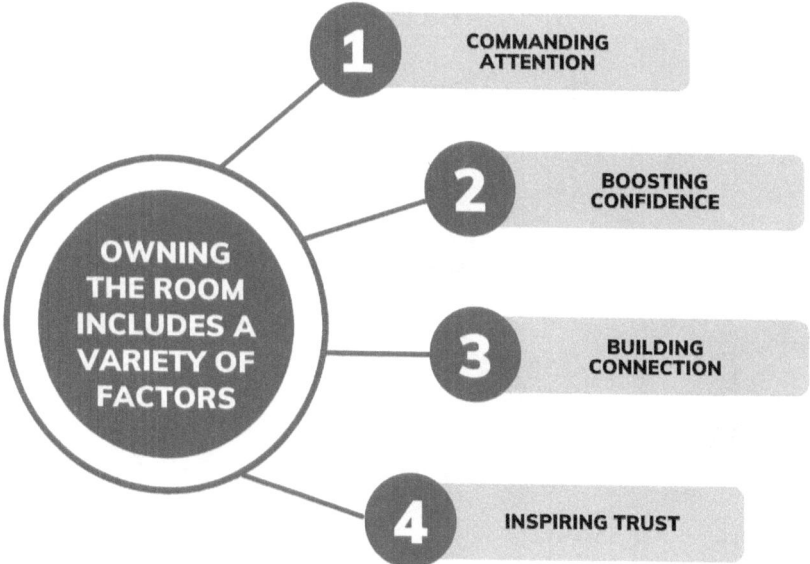

Now it's time to shift your focus to these four factors of owning any room:

Commanding Attention

Think about how you enter a room. You don't have to strike a pose, à la Madonna's "Vogue," but self-awareness is key. Most of us likely don't give this much thought in advance. We may brush our hair and straighten our jacket, which is a good start. But there's more . . .

Start by prepping yourself in a mirror. How's your posture? Can you look people in the eye? Do you have a smile on your face? Is your demeanor open and friendly? All of these things will help others see that you are leading the way in your conversation. While you're at it, ask a friend or colleague for their opinion too; it's always good to have a second pair of eyes.

Boosting Confidence

Recently, a colleague who was preparing for a big presentation asked for some tips to boost his confidence. "I'm a bit nervous," he said. "I don't know everyone in the room, and I'm a little worried." He's not alone—when I work with private clients and associations, one of the most common issues we work on is instilling confidence.

Of course, content is also key. You have to know what you're talking about inside out, upside down, and even sideways. If have a lot of confidence but little knowledge, it's just bluster. But you can also have a great deal of knowledge and expertise and still feel a little hesitant.

When I work with clients, I find that the area they need—and appreciate—the most help in is upleveling their confidence. It's the combination of confidence and content that boosts both your credibility and your presence.

 Tune in to my short video with my favorite tactics on how to boost your confidence in any presentation or conversation, get valuable intel before you start, and elevate your presence. These are tips leaders at all levels can use, right away.

Building Connection
Your overall goal is to create a concrete connection between you and your audience, whether you're chatting with your team, other leaders, a client, or even your friends. *This* is what will help them stay with you and buy into your message. After all, influence is all about getting someone to do something you want them to do and persuading them that they wanted to do it anyway.

Inspiring Trust
Trust is everything. If your audience doesn't trust you or believe you are both credible and authentic, they won't listen to you, and their level of buy-in will likely be nonexistent. When we think of how we can communicate clearly and influence others, trust and connection are at the starting gate. So start by determining how to earn their trust.

POWERING IT UP: YOUR FIRST STEP
Think about the best presenters you've seen. What makes them compelling, and exactly what made those presentations so successful?

I like to think of this as the "PLUS." If you attend a conference and rave about one of the speakers, most likely it's because of the relevant stories and examples they shared and the confidence, control, and credibility they exuded. They took the stage, but how did they do it? That's the PLUS factor you want to achieve: the executive presence.

Have you ever had what I call *mumble-itis*? If you have, you know what I mean. I was working recently with Jackie, a senior leader, in a group workshop on presentation skills. I'd noticed over lunch how personable she was and how she was always engaged in conversation. That changed in an instant! The minute she got in front of the group, she shrank within herself. Her arms were wrapped around her chest and her ankles were crossed. Her voice became so low and soft—mumble-itis—that I had to literally move right up next to her to hear what she was saying.

Face it, when you're not confident and haven't connected, your audience *feels* it. And when they feel it, you sense it too. And guess what? It only serves to make you more panicked.

When you're preparing for that all-important conversation, try this first: Stop and take an ever-so-slight pause. Then, quickly assess the room and the audience. The result? You'll be ready to rock.

You may be thinking that creating presence seems overwhelming; but truly, you can do it. Developing presence is part preparation, part visualization, and part mindset, and it starts with confidence. Jackie, for example, was absolutely capable of handling her talk and very knowledgeable about the topic, *but* she wasn't feeling confident—that's what derailed her. She felt everyone was looking at her (she was right, they were) and immediately focused on what she thought *they* might be thinking, instead of what *she* needed to convey. She was almost entirely stuck in her head.

Here's how I helped this executive solve the problem. Tack these two steps up on a Post-it or note right in front of your desk or computer so they come to mind easily.

DO YOUR HOMEWORK

I love the acronym DYH—Do Your Homework. Early on in my career, I worked in the real estate department for a grocery anchor tenant. One of my favorite leaders there started out bagging groceries and worked his way up to a leadership role.

Whenever we asked a question, he'd respond with "What have you found out? Do your homework!" He used this phrase often, and it's pertinent in almost every situation, even when you're not presenting.

This executive was able to develop deep perspective on all sides, from in-store roles to store development to leadership. Because he did his "homework," he learned how important both preparation and perspective were to ensuring the outcomes he wanted to achieve, whether he was conversing with his team or the board of directors. And he taught it to us—his team. We were, in fact, his audience.

If you don't know your own audience or understand how to effectively set the tone, your conversation can fall flat.

So before doing anything else, do your homework. You must be crystal clear on what message you are delivering and how you will get there successfully and effectively.

WORK THE ROOM

One way to do your homework when you're presenting or leading a meeting is to "work the room." This is a great method to create instant rapport and build trust. No matter what type of meeting or presentation you're in and no matter how large or how small your audience, there's almost always an opportunity to meet people as they enter. Take it!

Don't be afraid to introduce yourself! One way to do this is to ask a participant if they've been to this conference before and what they like about it. Then follow up by asking, "Jack, what do you especially want to hear about today?" Their responses will give you real-life intel about your audience and their expectations.

Working the room and inviting people to engage in advance makes them feel comfortable right away, and—bonus—it serves to relax you too and get you in the mode for your talk. What a good way to warm up any presentation or conversation!

FLEXIBILITY IS KEY

Sometimes, creating presence takes more than a little flexibility. When I first began presenting, I was invited to introduce the main speaker at a large conference. My job was to do this onstage at a podium and with a script (although neither the podium nor the script are my usual choices).

Because I'm a girl with a plan, I was eager to have a short rehearsal a few days in advance. We did—three times, actually. At our first rehearsal, the venue contact admitted they had a new AV system. She didn't know how to work it, and their usual AV person was out sick. She suggested we come back the following day, which was the day of the conference.

The next morning, I made sure I was at our room the minute the AV team arrived. But the crew (minus their usual expert guy) was busy setting up one of the main sessions and didn't have time to rehearse. Bada boom, time to punt!

Luckily, I was seated next to this speaker at lunch, and we had a great opportunity to chat. I always like to find out a little bit about someone that isn't in their bio or scripted information.

You can imagine what happened next: I climbed the steps to the stage and made my way to the podium. Thankfully, I didn't trip! Looking out at the audience, I saw only one big bright spotlight—on me. And I saw the very small light bulb on the podium, positioned directly over my script, flicker and sputter out just as I arrived.

Fortunately, because I had talked informally with the speaker (my Plan B), I stayed calm and relaxed. I didn't need my notes, and I knew enough about the speaker to make my introduction conversational. What did this do? Even though I wasn't the main speaker, I was able to gain the audience's attention from the start, and this set the tone. Had I not had a Plan B and had I *not* appeared confident, my presence would have been zero.

WHEN YOU WANT TO COMMAND ATTENTION

Prepare in advance, then let it go. Your audience can read information for themselves; your job is to help them understand what's between the lines or what hasn't been said. It's your insight that's key.

Have that Plan B, and a Plan C, and even a Plan D. Stuff happens, whether it's a physical issue—the light burns out, you trip on your way to the stage—or a faux pas. And unless it's egregious, there's no need to apologize; once you do, people start wondering what else may require an apology.

When You Want to Create Rapport and Trust

Personalize it. I find it's most helpful when I can create rapport before the meeting or presentation. I call this the "meeting behind the meeting." For example, if I'm meeting with a different team about a proposed budget or sales pitch and need their buy-in, I like to have a conversation first, before the actual meeting.

How long you spend with them isn't important—it can be a short time. The point is that using a personal touch adds to your ability to convey presence and, most importantly, builds trust. If you already know them, this will remind them of who you are and that they want to hear what you have to say. If you don't know them, they will be pleased at the introduction and you'll have a friendly face in your audience.

When You Want to Build Connection

Keep it coming. You've taken the first steps to build rapport and command attention. Now you have to keep it going. A great way to do this is to ask someone's name and use it—people love it, and there's nothing better than creating and continuing that connection. Whether I've been chatting with someone before a presentation or they've asked a question during a session, I always try to use their name as much as possible. If you can't make out someone's name tag or you knew their name and have momentarily forgotten it (it happens), just ask them—and be sure to repeat it. They will be pleased you asked.

— CHAPTER 3 EXERCISE —

Try this at home (or in your office) to amp up your presence. Go ahead, grab your phone—it's time to do a self-video. Stand up and talk about any topic you like for just one minute. Don't worry about the tech. Don't do a lot of takes.

I know one minute can seem like a long time but stick with it. You'll see what this exercise can do for you. When you're finished, take a moment to write down just two things:

· What you did really well
· Where you can do even better

This will give you a clear snapshot of how you can improve. Perhaps you're swaying side to side or playing with your jewelry, or you have your hands in your pockets. I use this self-video technique all the time when I'm coaching individuals and teams, and it really works!

CHAPTER 4
PREPARATION: IT'S YOUR SECRET SAUCE

AVE YOU EVER BEEN TO AN IN-N-OUT BURGER? THEIR SERVICE is legendary (as are their fries). If you're lucky enough to have eaten there, you know what I mean. In fact, the food is so good that it inspires true In-N-Out devotees.

Why? The key is their special sauce. It's creamy and tangy, and it has a little razzle-dazzle compared to other fast food chains. You could describe it as heaven on a hamburger, or on fries.

Now (maybe while you're munching on those fries), think about how you can create your own "special sauce" to help you in your next presentation. Sometimes, the most unexpected experiences are exactly your secret sauce to a successful presentation.

You may be surprised, for example, at how an early career experience made all the difference in how I prepare today and how it can help you. When I was twenty-one, I graduated from the University of Southern California armed with a theater degree but no job. My dad was quick to offer his advice: "Look for a job that pays!"

I walked into what was then called a personnel agency to see what they had to offer. Immediately, a woman handed me a checklist listing fifteen different types of office equipment; my task was to check off the ones I could operate proficiently. There was nothing else on the list.

Despite her prodding, I checked off . . . absolutely zero. My best skills weren't on that list, and I had bigger ideas. Apparently, however, mastery of that equipment was more important than brainpower, creativity, or the capability to lead.

I don't remember what this woman looked like or what she wore, but I do recall clearly what she said. She quickly ushered me to the door, looked me straight in the eye, and said, "You're nothing but another pretty face. You'll never amount to anything." (Ahem!)

I mustered all the confidence my then twenty-one-year-old self could deliver, looked right back at her, and replied, "Watch me." Then I marched (well, stomped) out of that office. By the way, this is a true story—you just can't make this stuff up!

Here's the surprise: I'm grateful to this woman for essentially telling me no. Unwittingly, she helped me see that determination, confidence, and—you guessed it—preparation really do make all the difference, both professionally and personally. I didn't know it then, but I learned an early lesson in how to be prepared and poised for things that didn't necessarily go my way.

You may feel you can't have that conversation with your team, talk with your child's sports coach, or answer questions in front of your leadership because you don't have the "right" background, but you can. Doing your homework in advance is key.

You may feel you can't possibly moderate a panel, ask your boss for a raise, or speak in front of a group, small or large, but you can. Building your confidence—and actually putting it into practice—is key.

Preparation makes all the difference. While it won't cover absolutely every situation, it offers a huge benefit when you're working on any presentation or conversation. If you're prepared, you'll know the structure and flow of your talk or conversation, you'll have a Plan B in your pocket in case anything changes or goes awry, and most importantly, you'll feel comfortable, poised, and natural when you talk.

TAKE BABY STEPS FIRST

Knowing exactly what to say and how to say it can be overwhelming. Perhaps you're getting ready to lead your first meeting or give your first presentation, and your inclination may be to just hurry and "get it done." While this approach could save you time on the front end, you probably won't love your results.

Consider That Secret Sauce

Start by considering what your own recipe for success will be. Ask these questions:

- What will make you stand out as uniquely you?
- What will help people remember your message?

As you prepare, weave these ideas or concepts throughout your presentation. For example, my special sauce is that I'm approachable and relatable. Clients can see I've been in their seat and understand the communication issues they face every day. And they can see that I can help them solve those issues and help their teams grow.

Another part of my secret sauce is that I'm not afraid to chat about mistakes I've made in presenting and what I did or didn't do. As I was writing this chapter, I received a comment on a post I'd done that featured a complete blooper!

 I was filming some short clips in between conference presentations. My excellent videographer caught me right on point: I couldn't manage to get what I wanted to say out of my mouth the way I planned! I was supremely tongue-tied. It took me a while to get it straight. This just shows it happens to everyone, and it does take effort to be effortless.

When she saw my post, this leader thanked me for showing my human side and providing a little laughter along the way. The best part? She really was impressed with my in-person presentation, and seeing this blooper made her like me even more.

Secret sauce? You bet.

Learn from Other Presenters

This is the perfect way to start out if you're new at presenting or want a refresher. Bring a notepad with you, and most importantly, think about *why* they were successful!

Ask these questions:

- Did the presenter engage you from the get-go?
- What hook or opening message did they use?
- Was their special sauce evident throughout?

Here's the thing:

Sometimes people think they'll pick up a few pointers and walk away being the best presenter ever, which could be true. However, in a way it's like being a hairstylist. If you have short, curly hair, I can't make it long and straight in an hour.

But I can give you tactics to get you there and describe how long it may take.

Sometimes we think the answer is complex—there's magic or a complicated equation in there somewhere.

But it isn't magic or rocket science; it's a process. It takes doing your homework, being organized, and practicing! When it comes to being a great presenter, here's my equation for success:

$$ \text{DYH} + \text{GET ORGANIZED} + \text{PRACTICE} = \text{PRESENTATION SUCCESS} $$

As leaders and managers, sometimes we underestimate the value of improving our sales skills. Maybe we aren't actually in a sales role, or we don't lead pitches often. But we all communicate and persuade our clients, customers, and colleagues every day, and how we prepare is critical.

Consider this question:

Did the speaker or presenter "wing it," or did the presentation seem rehearsed?

This can be either a boon or a bust. Not long ago, I was preparing for a conference presentation, and the organizers allowed me to poll a selection of their membership, the majority of whom were senior leaders. I always prefer to talk in person or via phone when I can, so I called each of these members, all of whom graciously agreed to take a short survey.

One of the questions I asked was "Do you rehearse, and if so, how?" I was surprised that many of these leaders said, "No. I wing it!" When I asked why, several said they felt they knew their content well enough to punt. Others replied that they didn't have time to rehearse. Some even said they usually thought they were prepared—but sometimes weren't.

Put simply, a little bit of rehearsal makes a difference. But on the other side of the fence, there is such a thing as being *too* prepared. My client Alex was working hard to prepare a quarterly presentation to his own clients and asked for my help. I asked him to show me exactly how he planned to deliver his presentation when we met in person. This meant bringing along any notes he planned to use, having his slides or handout ready, dressing as he would for the meeting, and prepping in advance.

He arrived clutching an entire sheaf of notes: two legal pads crammed with notes on every page. He was afraid he'd forget something! When he got up to talk, he was so focused on reading his notes that we could see the concentration on his face but not his personality. He had so many notes that he inevitably lost his place—and the thread of the conversation. How could Alex have prevented this?

The first trick here is to prepare your thoughts in advance and write them down. You can use a simple pad of paper or a whiteboard. There's something about writing your thoughts down and doing an actual outline that (a) helps you with the flow of your presentation and (b) makes you remember it. You'll feel much more comfortable and conversational if you know what's supposed to happen next.

Then, once you've written that script or outline, forget it.

That's right, toss your script!

One of the worst things you can do is read your talk, whether it's an outline or notes. When you read it, we know it. We can immediately see it on your face and hear it in your voice, because focusing on your notes doesn't make your personality shine—it actually does just the opposite. Almost always, your voice levels off into a monotone, your eye contact diminishes, and we often can't see your face because you're looking at . . . your notes. Your message gets lost.

Now it's time to put doing your homework into play.
This applies to just about everything.

Remember Alex: He had so many notes, he lost track of them and his presentation. He also lost his audience. What was the issue? He knew his content, so it wasn't that. His presence was decent and he looked the part, so that wasn't it either.

This was the problem: He wanted so badly to ensure his corporate leadership team could see *he* knew what he was talking about that he wound up stuffing way too much into his presentation. He was thinking more about himself than about what his audience needed or wanted. The result? They disengaged pretty quickly.

It's nearly impossible to be everything to everybody, so organize your presentation to be sure it flows smoothly and you captivate your listeners. Like Alex, sometimes we want to include everything that could possibly be important. Don't do that! Remember that clearly deciding on your topic is critical. Your audience wants to know you have all the background for your presentation or conversation, but that doesn't mean they actually want to hear it all.

CORRAL YOUR IDEAS

Determining where you get your best inspiration can help you corral your ideas. Sometimes I find that my best ideas come when I'm not in the office! I once figured out the theme to an entire training conference while at the gym on the treadmill, with my earphones blasting my favorite tunes. I often go to a local coffeehouse early in the morning—there's something about the white noise in the background (and the caffeine) that helps clarify my thoughts about the presentation I'm working on. My colleague Karen makes notes of possible ideas and resources, then drops them into a file folder in her desk drawer. When it's time for her next presentation, she has a file full of inspiration at the ready.

OUTLINE YOUR THOUGHTS

Map it out.

Think of your outline as a road map. If you don't plan where you're going, you may get there eventually, but with a lot of bumps and potholes along the way. Now that you've narrowed down your topic ideas using my whiteboard hack, use the following tips to get your outline in gear.

My favorite way to map out what I want to say is to use what I call the Power of Three. I like using this method to prepare an agenda, for

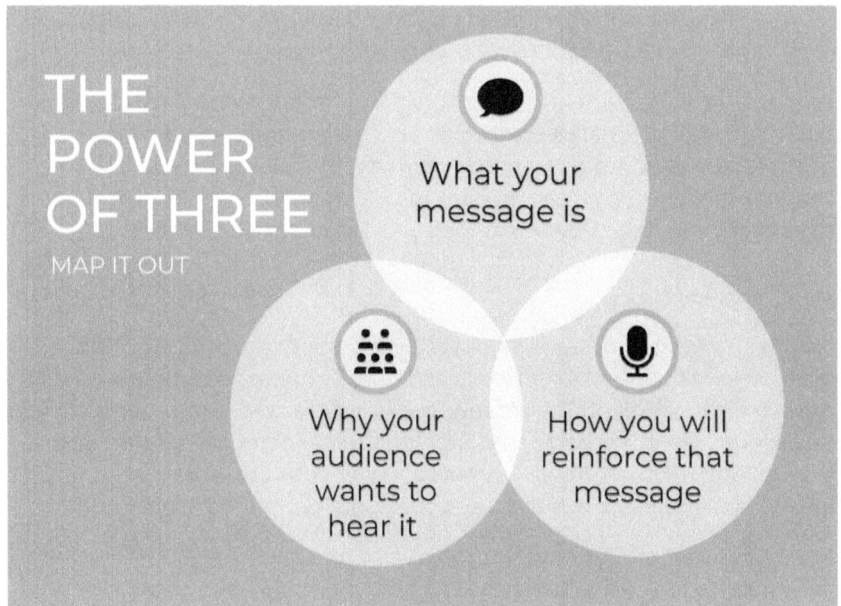

example, because it's repeatable, each and every time. It also forces you to focus on just three main areas.

Whatever method you choose, your goal should be to reduce the information you've researched into a keyword outline that will jog your memory but not keep you glued to your notes.

Break it down. Once you are finished jotting down your ideas, choose how you will outline and present a clear, coherent line of thought. Your eventual goal is to link all the elements of your presentation or speech together and demonstrate the connection between your stories or examples and your primary points.

Write it out. How much information is enough? Even though you have a lot to say, it usually isn't necessary to have it all down in print when you make your presentation.

This is the method that works most effectively for me: First, I jot down keywords that will remind me of what I want to talk about, such as "year-over-year sales" or "mission and values." I may even lightly color code my notes for my first draft; for example, I'll underline certain talking points I want to emphasize. Do *not* highlight or color code the

SHANNON ALTER

way you may have done in college! Try to highlight only the major points, or those you want to be sure to remember.

And just as actors rehearse their "blocking," or movement on stage, and note it in their scripts, I also note any movements I plan to make, such as crossing the room or stepping down from a platform. This ensures that my presentation goes as planned! A second benefit is that it helps me determine if the flow is smooth and logical when I rehearse.

EDIT RUTHLESSLY

Now is the time to bring out your inner editor. Go through the first draft of your outline with a fine-tooth comb, checking to make sure it's exactly right. Think of the last few books you've read. What parts did you skip? Most likely, the parts that didn't interest you or were otherwise boring, right? Do your own homework with your presentation— examine it and leave out the parts that bore people. Edit, edit, edit!

I also find it helpful to have someone else take a look—and a listen—to your outline to see if it flows smoothly to them. You don't have to make every change someone else recommends, but getting feedback is useful because you will be able to dial in on what goes over really well and what may need an adjustment.

Stay true to your material, your audience, and your personality. Audiences are smart: they will know right away if you skimp in any of these areas.

What if your style, or even your message, doesn't resonate with your audience? This is why researching your audience and supporting your facts in advance pays off. Doing your homework will also ensure the examples, stories, quotes, or statistics you include in are pertinent .

WHAT ABOUT MY SLIDES?

If you're planning to use slides, think about the look *and* feel of your presentation, and what you want the outcome to be.

My friend Jack asked me to take a quick look at his slides before an upcoming presentation. How many slides did he have, I asked, and how much time did he have for his presentation? Without blinking an eye, he replied, "Eighty-nine slides. For an hour."

I gulped. Trying to hide my dismay, I offered an alternative: less is definitely more.

Trust me, this is an important fact to consider if you plan to have slides of any sort. I like to think of it this way: our job as leaders (and presenters) is to not only communicate our topic but connect the dots for our audience. We're the translators.

First, consider your audience and your timing. What do they want or need to hear, and how much time do you have to get your message across? Remember, you'll need to tell them where they're going (your agenda) and how you'll get them there.

The workshops I do typically range from three hours to all day. They are always interactive and can include polls, role plays, "what if" scenarios, and other exercises—it all depends on my client's goals, our audience, and our timing. I do use slides for workshops because people like to take notes. However, I limit them as described below, and I use mostly images on the slides, with very little text, if any.

Beware of trying to cram too much in. People want to remember what you say, and if your slides are jam-packed with information, they won't remember it—or you.

The shorter your talk, the fewer main points and slides you should have. For example, if I'm giving a fifteen-minute talk, I'll have only one (or maybe two) points and corresponding slides.

For an hour-long presentation where the client or organizer requests or requires slides, or a longer immersive workshop where I think slides will be valuable, I may use more slides: around 20–23. You may or may not know at this point what the sequence of those main points should be (use that whiteboard!), but the important part is to begin firming up your thoughts and ideas. It's kind of like a puzzle: it's just a matter of fitting the right pieces into the right places.

TELL THE STORY

I call it the Exploding Engine Syndrome. I admit it, I'm not a car girl. I drive a Ford, which I love, and I hope that every morning when I get in and push the start button, it turns on. And if there's a problem and I need to take my car to the dealer for service, I usually like to see my reliable "car guy," Bob. When I bring it in at 9:00 a.m., Bob says, "Shannon, just wait here. I'll be back to you by 10:00 a.m. to let you know the GBU—the good, maybe the bad, and hopefully not the ugly. But in any case, I'll come find you by then."

Now, here's where the Exploding Engine Syndrome comes in. If Bob does what he promised—finds me by 10:00 a.m. and tells me the GBU—my shoulders relax. If, however, he doesn't get back to me on time and he's nowhere to be found, and it seems to be taking longer and even longer, what happens? I immediately wonder whether something more complex went wrong—for example, did the engine explode? Rationally, I know that's pretty unlikely, but when there's a lack of communication, my mind fills in the gaps!

This story illustrates what happens when communication in an organization is on the downslide, or even nonexistent. It's short, it's easy, it's relatable. And everyone can connect the dots.

When you're thinking about and organizing the stories and examples you want to use, jot down a few notes or bullets first to get them out of your head and on paper. Then, expand on each note to explain exactly how your audience will relate to your story. For example, my car story is a situation almost everyone of driving age can relate to. All you have to do is translate that familiar personal experience to a business example; the concept is the same.

People can read your slides and handouts for themselves. Our goal is to help people read between the lines and learn by hearing about what you've done. Be sure to weave in examples and stories throughout your presentation to illustrate and support your points and connect them throughout.

Suppose you're giving a talk highlighting differentiation as an important factor in delivering great customer service. I might illustrate my point with a story about the disparity in service I received from two airlines on the same day, or two different restaurants. This, too, is something everyone can relate to, and it is an excellent way to both reinforce the tone of your talk and provide a relatable example.

Remember, we always want to give our audience insight. Whether you are discussing potential sales, budgets, leading your team, or saving the planet, audiences want to know how what you learned can help them and what they can do with the information once they return to their offices or homes. Don't be afraid to include not only what you learned that worked but also what you tried that didn't work.

OKAY, I THINK I'M READY, BUT . . .

Imagine this scenario: you're feeling ready to make a business case to your boss, make a big pitch to a prospective client, or lead a crucial department meeting. You stand up, and . . . the words just fly out of your head! Worse yet, you realize your voice is shaky and you're having a hard time making eye contact.

What can you do? We'll address this in more detail in Chapter 8, but for now, take a peek at my short video for my two top tips to help you solve this, right back in your own office.

A SNEAKY SECRET: PREPARE FOR ANYTHING

I once had an employee who routinely filled in every hour of every day on her calendar with meetings and appointments. Not only was she clearly overbooked and seriously stressed, she also had no time for the unexpected. Realize that, no matter how precisely you have refined your speech or presentation, stuff happens. Your client changes his mind, the big boss decides on a different theme for your talk at the last minute, or the room setup isn't exactly as you expected. So no matter what, be sure to leave a little room for unforeseen events and out-of-the-blue issues.

The good news is that, while it's not possible to prepare for every eventuality, it is absolutely possible to handle any situation by using the tactics and techniques you're learning in this book. When you're prepared and have taken the time to practice, you will be more conversant and poised, and that confidence will be visible. You'll be ready.

TIMING IS KEY

What about timing? If anything could change, how do you know how long your final presentation will take? Understanding whether your timing will work is a key element to being ready to rock. This is true regardless of whether you're prepping for an actual presentation or a conversation. You'll only have a finite amount of time to get your point across.

When you're having a high-stakes conversation or making a crucial presentation, keep in mind that your audience wants to know:

- What the problem is
- Why they should care about it
- How you plan to resolve it and what your recommendation is

Here's an example of what can happen when you lose sight of your audience's needs:

I worked with a leader who, when asked to provide a business case or recommendation, was fond of adding multiple slides and documents. On one very long email, she included twenty-five attachments! Despite the long email, I didn't see a concise recommendation included— probably because she lost me after the first paragraph. I had no idea what the high points were or what she was asking for. I'm guessing she wanted me to review each of those twenty-five documents and come to my own conclusion.

Here's what to consider:

First, consider your background time. The time you'll need to prepare a presentation will depend on its depth and complexity. For a presentation that does not require a lot of research (the information and insight are coming out of your head), allow a minimum of four to six hours of preparation time for every hour of talk time. If additional research is required (e.g., Internet searches, phone calls, further reading) or you will be including music, photos, or videos, add on another two to three hours of preparation per each hour of talk time, plus any activities you plan to use.

Be sure to include enough time in your estimate to cover rehearsals. Rehearsing your material is important because it gives you the chance to examine the effectiveness of your phraseology, movement, timing, volume, and pace to see if it works well and flows smoothly. If at all possible, rehearse your presentation in front of someone else or in front of a video camera. Most likely you will find that you need to tweak a few areas—perhaps you want to emphasize a different point, include another story, or ask a thought-provoking question.

I use a timing sheet to record what I expect my timing to be. This is a really flexible tool that can be adapted for any communication. Examining your timing at this stage is crucial because when you do, you'll be able to better refine the hooks, stories, and examples you plan to use.

Here's the format I find most useful:

On each sheet, I list on the left (in the header): slide number (if I have slides), timing (exactly how long it takes), and slide topic. On the right side of the same sheet, I list any stories, examples, polls, or videos that I plan to use. I also include any applicable "homework." At the bottom, I simply add up the time for each section to be sure I'm on track.

I am diligent about filling out each part of my timing sheet. You can do this on your computer or write it down on paper; I like the latter because it's a visual reminder of what I've planned and how the flow will go. By doing this, I confirm and cement the ideas and what I want to say in my brain! And—bonus—I find that I don't have to use notes.

Here's an example of a timing sheet: I use this each and every presentation. It helps me determine whether the flow of my presentation is working, if the timing I have in mind is appropriate, and if my words sound the way I designed them to when I rehearse. I write this longhand because it's often quicker to make timing adjustments as I go, but you can easily fill out this template on your computer. Just be sure to use it while you're rehearsing!

SLIDE NUMBER	TIME	SLIDE TOPIC	STORIES/ EXAMPLES	ACTIVITIES
Section 1				
1	0.30	Title slide		
2	1.25	Video	What trips you up	
3	1.00	Intro		
4	5–7.00	Activity		(Activity name)
5–6	3.00	Challenges/ agenda		
Section 1 time	13.00			
7–9	2–3.00	Poll or hand-raiser		Poll
10	4.00	How to begin		
11	5.00	Activity		(Activity name)
Section 2 time	12.00			
Total time 1 & 2	25.00			

If you're doing a presentation with slides, list these headings across the top of your page:

- **Slide number:** Note the exact number of each slide you'll be talking about in the presentation (e.g., #1 or #1–3).
- **Time:** Write down the exact amount of time you think the slide or group of slides will take. I use the timer on my iPhone and go through every single slide. When you rehearse, do the same thing and amend any timing accordingly.
- **Slide topic:** List the main idea for each slide. For example, you could list "Title slide," "Introduction," "Challenges," and "Wind up."
- **Stories, examples, and activities:** Note each story, example, video, or poll you plan to use for each slide. Be specific. We'll address this in more detail in Chapter 8, but for now, take a peek at my short video."

You'll have a good idea of what to use and where to do so as you jot these ideas down. Don't worry if you aren't sure how they'll flow; you'll have the chance to refine this when you rehearse.

I like to tally up whatever I anticipate the timing to be. This gives me a preliminary idea of how everything will fit in and whether I've hit my main points. I use my Power of Three for this purpose: I consider each of my three main points a "section" and then note how much time I plan to allocate for each section. By doing this, you can also get a good visual on how any breaks or activities will work into your presentation.

By the way, I always ask the leader or organization I'm speaking for if they have planned breaks in mind. If the session is under an hour, it's likely not needed, but if you're doing a half-day workshop, for example, be sure to build them in.

— CHAPTER 4 EXERCISE —

Now's the time to paint the picture for your audience! In fact, once you cull down your ideas on the board, you can even put an image of it on a slide and bring it with you when you have that all-important conversation.

For this exercise, pull out your upcoming presentation or conversation and revisit the whiteboard hack described in Chapter 2. In that exercise, you used the whiteboard hack to help you decide on your topic; now you'll use it to organize each section of your presentation. The goal is to simply get all your ideas out of your head and onto paper, and I do mean all of them. Be sure to write down each separate idea on a Post-it and stick it up on your whiteboard, or even a desk, in no particular order. Then decide which ones pertain to the topic at hand, which to save for another topic, and which to discard. By getting all your ideas corralled in one place, you'll be able to see if you have too much—or even too little—for each section of your talk.

The key: don't hesitate to move or simply toss anything that isn't relevant or is just "too much stuff." Sometimes, we're afraid to move our ideas because we don't want to leave anything out.

Here's what I do to resolve that issue (plus, it makes me feel better!): I move ideas to the side if I don't think I can use them right away or am uncertain about them. I can always add them in later or use them in another talk. As the famous saying goes "Don't be afraid to kill your darlings!"

CHAPTER 5
HOOK 'EM: ENGAGEMENT IS THE KEY!

N OT LONG AGO, I DECIDED TO MAKE A THREE-LAYER CAKE from scratch. Dragging out my grandmother's *Modern Encyclopedia of Cooking*, published in 1955, I chose the butter layer cake recipe ("looks like pie, tastes like cake"). To my chagrin, I found out a little too late that a few pages were missing. The result was—you guessed it—a bit of a mess! The first layer sunk, the second stuck to the sides of the cake pan, and the third was, well, just a tad heavy.

What had I missed? In this case, I completely missed the cookbook author's helpful tips on the fourteen causes of butter cake failure! My point in relaying this story is that sometimes, when we're baking, we miss a crucial part of the recipe. And sometimes, when we communicate with our teams, we miss a critical part of the whole picture.

Our primary job is to tell the story, no matter what the topic. When you have a compelling opener, it grabs your audience's attention and makes them want to hear what comes next. Then, be sure to connect the dots and tie it all together.

Here's an example of what I call a "leadership meeting gone wrong," a situation that didn't work as well as intended for my colleague Alicia:

Alicia noticed that her team engagement at meetings needed a boost and asked me to sit in on the next meeting with her. The issue? She realized that very few people were responding to questions. There was a lot of whispering, and everyone seemed to be coming and going during the meetings. They just weren't paying attention.

She thought hard about implementing a new model and decided to invite three of her managers to lead the next one-hour meeting. The agenda would be up to them, and it would be their job to create buy-in and engagement. Alicia felt that since these managers were closer to the everyday action, it would be a surefire hit.

Did it work? Not so much. The managers Alicia assigned decided that they had a lot to say about what was—and wasn't—working well. And that's what they did! The meeting turned out to be more an information dump than an exchange or an opportunity to find out what their team was thinking.

Because these managers were so anxious to relay technical, task-oriented details about various processes, they began by displaying all their charts on-screen. Why did they choose this path? It was indeed in their comfort zone. *But* it was definitely not a conversation starter! In fact, it turned out to be a conversation inhibitor. While the presenters knew their topic, no one could decipher the hard-to-read charts or understand how the topic related to them. The audience checked out, right from the start.

Here's where this leadership team went sideways:

Their agenda was too long and comprehensive, and they tried to stuff too much into a one-hour talk led by three people. Face it, our brains can only hold so much information, particularly when it's technical or detailed in nature.

Try this instead: If you want people to remember what you said, focus on your most important items—the Power of Three—and be sure to include some breathing room. You can save the rest for another meeting or a follow-up Q&A.

Although the items they wanted to discuss were task-oriented, showing charts and spreadsheets on-screen is often a bust. It isn't engaging, and it's hard or even impossible to read. I don't put up a full spreadsheet unless it's required, and I always try to devise another way to convey the information first.

Try this instead: Extrapolate or pull out only the information you want your audience to see. If you're discussing department results with your CFO, or turnover with your HR group, put the highlights on the screen and let them stand out. You can always provide a handout before or after your meeting with additional information.

They didn't rehearse. This caused a few primary problems with their delivery:

- They discovered there was simply too much information to cover in the allotted time.
- They got off track repeatedly. After the meeting, I casually asked several employees what they thought were the main highlights— they didn't know!

WHAT'S YOUR HOOK? HOW TO CREATE AN OPENER THAT SELLS

We all sell, every day and in every way. Often leaders will say, "But I don't sell! I'm in operations." Or "I'm in the back of the house. I don't see anyone to sell to!" I disagree. As a consultant who helps organizations and teams communicate more clearly, I suggest that persuasion is indeed the name of the game, whether we're in a sales role or not.

And because we're persuading others to do what we want or need them to do, we've got to get them interested.

You may have guessed that I like to start things off with a bang! Crafting a creative opener accomplishes three things right away:

- Engages the audience
- Establishes a connection with them
- Offers a glimpse of what's to come

Remember that it's our job to tell a story that sticks and to connect the dots. Here are different types of hooks you can use to make an impact in your own presentation or meeting:

Use a Story
Start with a story or an anecdote. You'll remember the story I shared at the beginning of this chapter about making a cake from scratch, and how I tied that experience into helping leaders communicate better. Drawing on your own experiences instantly allows your audience to relate to you and encourages them to identify with your topic. I'll sometimes use a short video, either of myself or another person, to

illustrate my theme. Whatever story you choose, be sure to connect it to the rest of your message; otherwise, it's just a story.

Get Them Moving!

I like to get people up on their feet and moving right away. If time allows, I'll usually start with an activity and break them up into groups.

This accomplishes several things: It gets them talking, which is what I want them to do. It helps them get to know each other, if they don't already. And ultimately, it makes them feel more comfortable responding and more willing to contribute during the rest of the session. There's always a way to get people to talk—you just have to provide the direction and the opportunity.

Some people will naturally be comfortable speaking up in a larger group and some absolutely won't, but most people will be somewhere in the middle.

Try this: First, consider the room setup. I like a maximum of five people per group (if in rounds); any more than that can create sidebars. If the room is set up theater style, with everyone in rows, I simply say something like "Get on your feet! Turn to the person to the right of you. Turn to the person to the left of you. You three are a group!" It's easy, it works, and they love it.

Relay a Statistic

If you've got a telling statistic, flaunt it! For example, in a presentation on employee engagement, I might say, "Did you know that experts estimate over 68% percent of Americans aren't engaged in their jobs?" Or if I am meeting with a CFO or COO, I could say, "We reduced expenses on our office portfolio by an unexpected ten percent last month." If you use this type of opener, beware of burying your listeners in too much detail.

Think about the "gold nugget" in the message you're relaying. You should always be conscious of your audience and how much detail your topic requires. Remember that your CFO, for example, may be having similar conversations with other leaders, and their viewpoint may be necessarily broader.

Try this: Tell your leadership what the impact of your information is, or what will trip them up if they don't know it. That's the gold.

Ask a Question

I always ask the audience what they would like to learn from my program, and I always ask for their takeaways at the end of our conversation.

This gives me the opportunity both to hear what they think the program is about and to highlight the areas they are interested in during the presentation, if possible. It also allows me to check in on their satisfaction level at the end of the program and make sure they got what they came for.

This works with any size group; you just have to stay on track and lead them to where you want them to go. Asking up front what your listeners want to learn tends to work best with a smaller group (fewer than fifty people). To make this work with a larger group, enlist the help of an audience member in advance who is willing to provide an answer you want everyone to hear, thus reinforcing your message.

It's important to keep in mind that sometimes your audience may have lots and lots of questions or bring up something that's completely off topic. How you handle this depends on the type of talk you are giving and the time allotted.

Even though you may not always have an extended amount of time to give, most speakers are willing to stay after their talk to answer questions. If I am presenting a workshop that has breakout groups, I make my way around to each group so I can answer many of their questions in the smaller group setting.

Use a Quote

A good quote in your opener can be magical. It can immediately provide a picture for your audience of what you're going to talk about and how that topic relates to them. A quote can also reinforce your message, set the tone for your talk, and let your audience know that your ideas are well-supported.

> "The human brain starts working the moment you are born and never stops until you stand up to speak in public."
>
> **GEORGE JESSEL, COMEDIAN**

When I'm doing a workshop on presentation skills, I like to use a quote from old-time comedian, George Jessel. Everybody can relate to it, and it helps people realize they're not alone in experiencing that feeling.

You can also have fun with this by looking in your own backyard. I used to work for someone who was well-known in our company for quoting a lot of sayings, such as "You need them more than they need you," which I might use in a session on negotiating. I still use those quotes to this day!

Survey or Poll the Audience

A quick survey of your audience is easy to do and can yield lots of information. Depending on my audience, the topic, and the time available, I like to do this in a few different ways:

Advance survey: If a client or association allows it, I often send a preconference or premeeting survey. I purposely make it short, just three or four questions. It isn't scientific, but it gets my audience engaged before we actually meet and gives both me and my client some intel. When I do this, I always share the general results (e.g., "Seventy-five percent of us said . . .") and tie it into our conversation.

Poll: If the technology allows, I use a polling app, often while people are getting settled in their seats. It takes only a few minutes and has the side benefits of getting them engaged right away and giving them something to do. And they love hearing the live results or seeing them on-screen.

Hand-raisers: Sometimes the tech doesn't work or the internet fails. And sometimes what's old is new again. Go low tech and use an actual hand-raiser! Try it on almost any yes/no or either/or question. You can always elaborate on the answer.

You can also try this in an even more visual way.

In one all-day workshop I delivered, my client had relayed that the number of employees had risen dramatically over the past few years. To illustrate the many changes in the organization and their impact, I first asked all the employees who had been with the company a year or less to stand. Seventy-five percent of the group stood up.

I then asked employees who had been there for two years to stand up, and so on. By the time we reached the five-year mark, only two employees were left sitting. It was a quick, visual way to illustrate the amount of change in the organization in a relatively short time.

Other survey questions can be less dramatic but still revealing. For example, if you are giving a presentation on public speaking skills, ask for a show of hands to indicate how many people are in management-level positions and how many are in administrative-level positions. Or briefly ask your audience to name a few excellent public speakers.

These types of questions can help you further assess the audience, glean what they feel is important, and lead them right to what you want them to hear. This technique can also act as an icebreaker: employees or audience members now have a few topics to talk about with each other!

Provide a Call to Action

An easy way to do this is to give your audience a homework assignment. This keeps them listening and on their toes. And it serves to remind your audience about how they can use the great tactics you provided—whether back in their offices or at home. It also reminds them what a great speaker you are!

ANALYZE YOUR FLOW

Depending on what you read, it was either Plato or Agatha Christie who first said, "Necessity is the mother of invention," meaning we are prone to create a solution when there is a need. Either way, for me, the need was to develop a method to check my timing and confirm my stories and examples work the way I planned them when I rehearse.

I explained timing sheets in detail in the "Timing Is Everything" section of Chapter 4, so go back to that section now for a refresher on how to set one up. Give it a try on your next presentation!

— CHAPTER 5 EXERCISE —

My former boss loves the TV show *The Voice*. He's not a singer by any stretch of the imagination, but he loves this show. Why? There are characters you can root for. It's relatable. When he gives a presentation or has to relay information about financial performance or an employee issue, he does exactly that—he makes sure it's relatable.

When it comes to relatability, think of your job as the translator. It's up to you to successfully communicate and convey your message.

Try this: Go back to your agenda. Did you use the Power of Three to come up with your three main points? Do you have too many subheadings or smaller points listed? Write down exactly the three points you want to convey, with no more than three subpoints underneath. Then adjust for timing.

Connect your stories and examples. Think of this as weaving a golden thread throughout your presentation. You may have a great story, but if you don't connect the dots, it's just a story. For each story or example on your timing sheet, jot down how it connects with your main theme.

Try this instead: This one is easy—rehearse × 3! Not everyone is a great speaker. Practicing in advance pays off. This will not only allow you to check your timing and physical presence but assess who is the best fit for each area of discussion. You'll also feel more comfortable and have a better sense of the flow you want to achieve.

CHAPTER 6
IMPOSTOR SYNDROME:
BE THE EXPERT

N OT LONG AGO, I WAS SELECTED TO RECEIVE A PRESTIGIOUS industry award. This industry award is given every year to instructors who have demonstrated exceptional commitment to the advancement of professional education in the real estate management industry. This was a wonderful honor, and I was delighted to receive it!

Here's where the *but* comes in. You may be surprised at the *why*. Every year I try to attend this association's conference, but I rarely attend the awards banquet, where all awardees are publicly congratulated and given their actual physical award. For someone like me, who loves to be up on almost any stage, you'd think this would be a bonus.

I can get up on a stage (or no stage), speak in front of audiences of five people or a thousand, and have an easy, flowing, and flexible conversation with groups of people I've never met, all without batting an eyelash. *But*, I don't love having the actual focus only on me.

Why not? Here's the list I came up with; yours may be the same:

- A lot of new people I didn't know would be there.
- What if people thought I didn't deserve the award?
- Would anyone be envious?
- Who would I sit with?

- Was I wearing the right clothes?
- How would the photos turn out?
- Couldn't I just do this virtually?

You can see where I'm going with this. I was so nervous about what turned out to be a smidge of time onstage that I was clenching my jaw! And I train, facilitate, and speak in front of others for a living, so this was unusual for me.

So, what went sideways? You guessed it: impostor syndrome. I was my own worst critic.

Would I have been more relaxed if I'd used my own tips and tricks for communication and presentation skills? Definitely. I could have taken a breath (or a few). Here's what I did do: I found a few friendly faces, joined their conversations, and asked for introductions.

GETTING STUCK IN YOUR HEAD

Anything can happen to derail us, anytime—no matter what your conversation or presentation is. We forget what we want to say, people ask unusual questions, the tech falls apart, your outfit doesn't fit in. For many of us, this results in being stuck in our own heads!

Here's the good news: if this sounds familiar, you're not alone. In fact, it's pretty common. You'd be surprised how many expert professionals I meet in a variety of industries who have had similar experiences. Overcoming this is critical when it comes to presentation skills and communicating well, because we want others to perceive that we are both experienced and well-spoken. We want to be able to influence them. And sometimes, we even want to be perfect.

If you aren't familiar with impostor syndrome, it's when we doubt our own abilities and talents, especially when we're high achievers used to doing well. *Psychology Today* estimates that 70 percent of adults have experienced impostor syndrome at some time. The American Psychological Association adds that this phenomenon can even lead us to feel others will find out we're not as good as we thought, or that we're a "fraud"! When good old doubt creeps in, it can almost immediately undermine our confidence *and* our ability to be influential.

BURNING QUESTIONS—AND SOLUTIONS

I was leading a persuasive communication workshop recently and asked participants what their challenges were. I like to do this in every presentation because it engages them right away and gives me on-the-spot intel on what they're looking for. Immediately, a hand shot up. This participant was so excited she almost shouted out her answer! "I've been bursting to tell you," she said. "I think I know what to say in advance, but then it gets jumbled. I'm worried people will think I don't know what I'm talking about."

You, too, may have a list of burning questions about how impostor syndrome affects your daily communication and how you can use it to your advantage. My friend Janice is an experienced leader, but she still gets nervous. She's in a women's group where they share advice and personal experiences about leadership. After listening to a conversation, she said, "No wonder! I experienced *exactly* that! I just wasn't familiar with the term."

I think we all have burning questions on impostor syndrome, especially when it comes to speaking in front of others. If you're like me, you'd rather completely avoid the topic! I'm often asked how presenters, both new and experienced, can tell what their trigger points are and what they can do to help themselves.

In my experience coaching leaders, this has everything to do with confidence, having your Plan B in place, and remembering what *you* do well.

For example, my client Stephanie is very personable when she interacts with her team. But when it comes to presenting her team's results up the ladder to her boss and her boss's boss, she just melts. This is good old impostor syndrome lingering in the background! She wants so badly to impress them and show she knows her stuff that she actually comes across in the opposite way.

When I asked Stephanie why she felt her presentation had to be perfect, she thought about it for a moment and said, "If I don't do that, my executive leadership will see that I don't know what I'm talking about." Actually, it's just the opposite. They will appreciate your sharing just the right amount of information to allow them to take action or make an informed decision. Remember that sometimes, less is indeed more.

Here's why: Stephanie does know her stuff, but she over-prepares by piling in as much background information as possible, in chronological order. She wants it to be 100 percent perfect. When I dug a little further, she said, "It needs to be perfect because I *should* know!"

As a result, (a) Stephanie's audience can't digest what she's saying because there's simply too much information, (b) she loses them, and (c) her confidence takes a big hit. She winds up feeling even more stressed and anxious. You may feel this, too, when you've covered everything but aren't getting the results you want. Whenever you catch a glimmer of this, jot down when and where you felt that way. You'll be better able to anticipate any triggers the next time you present.

When we think about how we can persuade and influence others, consider this: your job is to communicate clearly and focus on the areas your audience wants/needs to know.

DON'T GET BOGGED DOWN IN DETAIL

People do want to see that we know our stuff. *But* that doesn't mean we need to include every last bit of information. When we do that, our audiences can get . . . well, bored! Sometimes, we want to include a *lot* of detail, and that's where we start. Unfortunately, this can lead to becoming mired in all that detail—we're stuck right in the middle.

Instead, tell them what they need to know and how it impacts them. Consider what will impact them or their decision the most—that's influence.

It doesn't always need to be 100 percent perfect! I think our teams and audiences actually appreciate when we're not because it makes us seem human and real.

Try this: When you're doing your homework, write down or highlight the two or three items your audience wants/needs to know. This applies whether your "audience" is your own leadership team, your child's teacher, or an association meeting. Give them the good stuff first: tell them what will help them or what may trip them up.

Then, reinforce your message. This is key, because even if you mention a particular concept or tactic once, someone will almost always chime in with "What did you say?" or "What was that thought?" and you'll need to repeat it anyway. If you plan how you'll reinforce your message throughout, your ideas and tactics will likely stick with them. As legendary sales speaker Dale Carnegie said, "Tell the audience what you're going to say, say it; then tell them what you've said."

Keep the rest of the information you've put together in your virtual "back pocket." You'll instantly feel more comfortable and confident because you have at your disposal more great facts, figures, and examples when you need them.

TACTICS AND TIPS TO OVERCOME IMPOSTOR SYNDROME

Not surprisingly, impostor syndrome can show up unexpectedly in all areas of life. Here are some of the best tactics and tips I've used to help leaders and executives solve those concerns and come out on top. You can use these too, every day.

Recognize the Signs of Impostor Syndrome

Picture this: You're feeling like you have to over-deliver or explain everything in order to be considered an expert and earn people's trust.

■ **Why this happens**

Take a good, hard look at the first draft of your presentation. If, for example, you discover that you have a hefty number of slides, it's time to go back and edit, and even delete. You may be thinking, No! I can't possibly delete anything! What will I say?

■ **If this happens**

You're planning to present a portfolio performance report to your leadership team, and you've been advised you'll have only twenty minutes. You take a second look at your presentation and—gulp— you have fifty slides, and they are crammed full of info. You've over-prepared.

■ **Try this**

Think about your goal: what do you need to get across, and how can you make it smooth and easily understood by your listeners?

1. First, get laser-focused on the Power of Three. Go back to your agenda and make sure you've listed only your top items. For a twenty-minute talk, focus on one or two items at most. You can have a third item on hand, if needed. Time flies, and you'll be both pressed and pressured if you try to include more.

2. Second, hide the slides or text you've decided not to use. This way, you'll still feel comfortable that you have the information if you need it; they are in your back pocket. If I'm not certain whether I'll change things around, I may do just this. If I am confident that I don't need those slides, I'll delete them.

3. Third, don't apologize! Unless something egregious occurs, don't apologize. When you do, it's all too easy to get flustered. And when you do, your audience wonders what else they may have missed that you didn't apologize for. For example, say you planned to include a point and forgot it, or ran right past it. When you point it out, you may appear disorganized and your audience may get confused.

Hot tip: Remember that in most cases your audience *doesn't* know exactly what you've planned to say. Typically, you can either bring that point in later if it's important, or you can let everyone know you'll be pleased to discuss that after your meeting or session. If they want to know more, they'll ask.

By the way, if someone compliments you on your presentation, take that wonderful compliment graciously and thank them! Sometimes it just isn't necessary to be 100 percent perfect, and the feedback you receive may be better than you expect. I was delighted, for example, by a viewer's comment on a blooper reel I posted: "The best way we can walk through life is having a good laugh at ourselves . . .Thanks for being real!"

Learn to Manage the Symptoms

Picture this: You're up in front of that room, leading your first client or association meeting. You know establishing yourself as an expert is critical, so you include a slide listing all your accomplishments and awards. In fact, you use two slides. Or you pull out your CV and read it (this happens!). You notice everyone is looking down or at their screen, not at you. You're also beginning to sweat. You're clasping and unclasping your hands. Your voice is suddenly higher and sort of screechy.

Why this happens: When we feel out of control or as though we don't know what will happen next, we often gravitate to what's familiar: ourselves, or our backgrounds and accomplishments. I know that people can google me or look at my website or LinkedIn to see my background, so I give them only the best stuff when I introduce myself. If you put too much in, people won't remember it; but they will remember the highlights. Your credibility as an expert will speak for itself.

Try this: First, take a breath. Really. We'll discuss more about body language later, but you can try this tip now. If you notice you're talking faster and faster, for instance, or finishing too early, you can wind up feeling rattled. Practice taking a pause. As long as it's short, people won't notice, and it will give you a moment to collect yourself and slow down. I guarantee this tactic is a surefire winner! You'll feel more confident, right away.

Second, consciously practice modulating your voice and articulating. If your voice tends to be a little high, try lowering your voice to make it sound smoother. Think of this as what author and hostage negotiator

Chris Voss calls using your "late-night DJ voice." This encourages your audience to actually listen to you. If your voice is too soft, people won't listen because they can't hear you. When you can't hear a speaker, it's mostly just annoying and you may tune out. Practice specifically adding variety and volume to your voice.

Work with Impostor Syndrome When It Shows Up

You and your boss are in a meeting with your most important client. Even though you know your stuff upside down and sideways, your boss takes over the conversation, simply because he knows the client well and they've worked together for a long time.

During the meeting, you can't stop thinking about what you can do to insert yourself. Afterward, you ruminate over every small detail and end up fatigued and overwhelmed.

Why this happens: When we're so busy thinking about what we *should* say and what isn't going well, we don't really listen to the conversation. We miss valuable opportunities to contribute and leave feeling we didn't deserve to be there—classic impostor syndrome.

Try this: First, remember what you do well and focus on it. You're there for a reason, and people want to hear what you think. Your job is just to translate it.

Second, get out of your own head. When Jessica and I worked together, I coached her on how to boost her confidence by finding and using her own "walk-in music." This is truly the best secret you can use. I use this technique in two ways, and you can too:

Start with walk-in music that gives you a spark! If I'm speaking to a larger group, either on a panel or for a workshop or keynote, I play a selection of lively tunes as people are walking in. I tend to play upbeat, fast-paced tunes from the '60s or '80s because they are fun and lively. I admit I like it loud—even if I can't blast tunes right before a meeting because it's more formal or I'd be disturbing others, I still play it right before I step into that meeting.

This accomplishes two important things:

1. Have you ever walked into a room that's too quiet? It can be a conversation killer! Walk-in music allows people the freedom to chat with each other and they feel relaxed, which is what you want. After all, your goal is to get them to interact with each other and with you.
2. It will make you more relaxed too, and it's fun!

— CHAPTER 6 EXERCISE —

We may not always be able to completely overcome impostor syndrome quickly. However, practicing these tactics can help you turn it around.

My favorite tactic to use when I coach clients is to bring out your phone! It's time to revisit self-videos, which I introduced in Chapter 3. Try this before your next presentation:

1. Record part of your presentation, voice only. This is so you can hear exactly how you sound. Think about whether you're speaking too quickly, whether you're breathing, and how low or high your voice is. If you notice there seems to be no punctuation in your talk, it's time to slow down.

2. Graduate to doing a quick self-video. Talk about anything you like that is familiar to you (work-related or not) for one minute. I recommend doing this yourself, rather than having a friend or spouse video you. This decreases the pressure you may feel when someone is watching you and makes it feel less like a performance. Don't worry about whether your lighting is on point, the camera is getting the best shot, etc. What's important is that you get to practice and can see yourself. I know, I don't always love watching myself on camera either. But the benefits are huge!

Are you using the influence you have? To tackle impostor syndrome and communicate persuasively, try these must-have tactics. After you do these exercises, write down the results of your practice so you can gauge your progress. It's easier than you think.

CHAPTER 7
CONQUERING THOSE JITTERS: GET GROUNDED

WHEN I'M LEADING A WORKSHOP FOR A CLIENT, I ALWAYS like to survey the participants in advance, or I'll do a poll right there in the workshop. This serves several purposes: It shows both me and my client what the participants are thinking about. Most importantly, it gives employees and attendees the opportunity to share their greatest difficulties or obstacles when giving a presentation or leading a meeting.

One question I always ask is "What makes you the most nervous when it comes to presenting or leading a meeting?" It's actually the most popular question—everyone can relate to it! People usually want to share their experiences of having the jitters, and they want to find solutions. My goal is to help them become cool, calm, and composed in any conversation or presentation, by using the tactics they learned in this book.

As my grandma used to say, "You have to figure out what the hitch in your get-along is first." To me, that means taking a moment to pause and determine what's stopping you from being successful in your presentation, meeting, or pitch.

Sometimes it's confidence or just plain old nerves. Often we're worried about what others may think of us. One high-profile executive I coached was anxious about his tendency to blush. "I can tell I'm turning bright red, every time," he said. "Once it starts, I don't feel very confident in what I'm saying, and I stumble. I just know everyone is looking at me, and it feels like they are staring, even if they're not. I don't feel I'm conveying the influence I'd like to."

It's difficult to be poised when you're stuck in your head, worrying the whole time about how you look or sound. I worked with this executive on his challenge by helping him simply become more flexible. Soon he could pivot adeptly when he needed to—in other words, he learned to roll with the conversation and own it when he felt himself blushing. Both of these tactics helped him relax, and his tone became more conversational almost immediately. He was better already!

When I was in high school, I loved to act and dreamed of being an actor. The "hitch" for me was that I wasn't very good at memorizing lines. I was deathly afraid I'd forget my lines and there I'd be, standing silently onstage with the audience staring at me, waiting. What a nightmare!

I wasn't used to being in front of a big audience, but I wanted to be, so I devised what was certainly a short-term solution: I wrote the important words (think bullet points) from my script —on my hand. As you can imagine, that didn't really solve the issue. I didn't have much room and couldn't read my notes anyway in the dim stage lighting. It made me feel better at the time, but it's hard to be charismatic when you're focusing on reading your notes, in any format.

That solution was clearly not meant to last! Even if the playhouse stage isn't your next stop, you can try the following steps to turn your anxiety into assurance and influence in your next presentation. When you're working to ease the jitters, start here:

DETERMINE WHAT YOUR "HITCH" IS

You may already be aware of what gives you cause for pause or makes you stop in your tracks when you're presenting or leading a meeting.

If you're not sure, jot down a few notes on what you *think* gives you the jitters and then what *actually* did. These prompts will get you going:

- I forgot what I was saying.
- I didn't know anyone in the audience.
- I dropped my notes!
- I talked too fast and was done way too early.
- I thought I was speaking loudly, but people couldn't hear me.

66

STOP WORRYING ABOUT PERFECTION

Sheryl Sandberg said it best: "Done is better than perfect." This absolutely applies to that important conversation we're about to have, when our nerves are bristling as we try to decide how to make it just right.

I was chatting with a colleague recently who was worried about a presentation she had just given. "I don't think I was very persuasive," she said. "I got off track—I just know everyone was looking at me. This always seems to happen."

Does this sound familiar? The key here is to not obsess. Often we set super-high expectations of ourselves (i.e., we expect to be perfect) or misinterpret what others think or expect. And then we obsess even more because we feel everyone's eyes on us.

That, in turn, sticks in our brains, creates pressure, and makes us even more nervous than we already are.

It's true, the participants in your presentation or meeting *are* looking at you—they want to hear what you have to say. Like the Nike slogan says, sometimes you have to "Just do it" and get over the fact that people will be looking at you.

Here's a secret tip: train your brain to be nonstick. If you get off track, keep it rolling. Most of the time your audience won't realize you've forgotten something, your timing is off, or you missed an example or story. And most of the time, you may be able to weave it back in or follow up with a pertinent question.

CONNECT WITH YOUR AUDIENCE

I was chatting with a colleague after a meeting when she asked, "How can I be more relatable? I feel I'm friendly, but I always get stuck in the introductions, and I'm not sure what to do."

I discovered what is now my number one tactic to be both relatable and authentic in front of any audience. You've got to connect with them first, and a great way to do that with any group, large or small, is to just talk with them. I call it "working the room." Be sure to refer back to Chapter 3 for more details on this topic.

Here's the key: Start *before* your meeting or presentation. It's all about how you make those connections, right from the start. Check out my quick video here—I used this to set the tone for my session on persuasive communication at a national conference.

Make your introduction simple. People can read your CV or bio and see almost everything they need to know about you in a conference brochure or online. What they want is to get to know *you* and the energy, confidence, and relatability you bring to the table.

I like to greet people when they're walking in and say hello, welcome them, and chat for a moment. If you're a natural networker, you may already be doing this. But somehow it can seem easier when you're part of the audience and not at the front of the room!

Guess what? When you use this tactic, it instantly makes your audience comfortable with you, and you with them. Those jitters disappear—which is what we all want!

KNOW YOUR MATERIAL

Simply put, you have to know your material backward and forward. Being completely familiar with your topic and your talk allows you to be more comfortable, confident, and conversational, period.

A side benefit is that you're less likely to be rattled if something does go amiss. No matter where you are, stuff happens: the power goes out, your client is late, the audiovisual guy doesn't show up, your materials don't arrive. You get the idea.

Is there a downside to knowing everything you want to say perfectly? Actually, yes. I was chatting with a friend about this very chapter, and I asked her what aspects of public speaking rattled her the most. She quickly said, "I want to know everything. And I feel like I need to use it all!" This can result in an unintended glitch: our presentation or talk can feel forced and scripted.

I like to quote experts when it adds to the conversation, and I'll add one of my own here: It takes a lot of effort to be effortless!

It may take a little while (and a bit of rehearsal), but your goal is to know your topic and your talk so well that you can discuss it without being tied to your notes. I know, that can be a scary proposition! That sturdy podium in front of us and our notepad or sheaf of notes can turn out to be a crutch—exactly what we want least.

USE A PRESHOW ROUTINE

Perhaps this situation has happened to you: You're attending an all-company meeting and your boss asks you to fill in for another speaker—a mere twenty-four hours before presentation time. You whip together a quick but hopefully complete presentation and announce that you're ready to roll.

Up on stage, you begin delivering your message, only to realize in the middle of it that some points aren't coming out of your mouth in the way you intended. In a rush, you trip over your words and your confidence plummets.

It's a fact that when you're up in front of a group, some points come out differently than the way you imagined and differently from what you scripted. That's because what's on paper or on your computer screen doesn't always sound the same when spoken out loud. The remedy? Routine and rehearsal are key, even if your time is limited.

I find it helps to do certain things in the same order every time I speak, both prior to my talk and during it. Just as a golfer or other pro athlete sets a preplay routine in place, so should you. Having my own pregame routine also helps quell any jitters!

TAKE A BREAK

When your audience is restless, things can go downhill in a hurry. That alone can make us even more nervous. Thankfully, no one in any of my presentations or meetings has fallen asleep yet! Keeping clients, employees, colleagues, and other audiences engaged is our job, and you can do this by using the tactics and tips described in this book. If they are engrossed in what we're saying, that makes us more confident.

Sometimes, taking a break—physical or figurative—makes everyone feel more comfortable. It can clearly position you as the leader and the person in charge. If, for example, you notice more people are getting up to use the restroom or using their phones, it's time for at least a quick stretch break. If you don't have time for a longer break or are concerned that people may not come back quickly enough, you can ask everyone to stand and take a quick three-minute stretch. Note that it may actually be five minutes—things always take longer than expected—so include that in your timing.

Another way to do this is to rearrange the seating. Of course, this will depend on the length of your presentation and on your audience. If you're meeting with your C-suite team, for example, it's unlikely that you'll be directing where they sit. However, if you're leading a team training meeting or facilitating a larger presentation, sometimes rearranging the seating will get people going and refresh their interest.

I find this works best when done before a planned activity or after a break or lunch. It's key to let people know it's coming and to be ready for the change, as they may leave their belongings at their seats.

MAKE SURE EVERYONE CAN HEAR YOU

I'm sure you've had this experience: You're at a conference or meeting and all is going well. You're looking forward to hearing the next speaker. But when that person begins to speak, you can't hear them. It could be that the room is big or you're at the back, but all you know is you want to be able to hear them and it isn't happening. You begin to tune out. Worse yet, perhaps you leave the room.

If you've ever been to a presentation where you cannot adequately hear the speaker, it's irritating. And that's just if you're an audience member. If you're the speaker, you're not conveying your message clearly, and you're definitely not influencing your audience the way you'd like to. It can be a bust, and, boy, can it increase those jitters.

Often, it's a question of awareness. Leaders who are new to presenting in front of others may not realize their voice doesn't carry the way they think it does. And often, even experienced leaders feel they've "got it down" when they actually don't. Perhaps they haven't been able to practice in front of others or record themselves and don't realize what's missing: their voice.

To ensure this doesn't happen, try these tactics:

■ **Use a Microphone**
Make it easy for people to hear you. My voice carries well, but my rule of thumb is that I always ask for a mic (preferably a lavalier mic) if there are over fifty people in the room or the facility is especially large. Reduce that number if your voice tends to be softer or lower. And be sure to actually try it out before you get up in front of the group.

Then, even though I always rehearse in advance, I ask a friend or colleague to stand at the back of the room so I can do my own "sound check," whether I am wearing a mic or not. If they can't hear what you're saying, it's a sure bet no one else will.

■ **Repeat the Question!**

I was at a presentation recently where the speaker asked for questions after his presentation. This was a great idea, except there were no microphones in the audience or on the tables. This can be a challenge because even though people want to ask questions, their voices may not carry well or be too soft. In this example, every time someone asked a question, the speaker replied directly to the attendee.

The problem? No one else heard the question, or the response. This made it difficult to determine what the speaker was responding to, and the exchanges became almost one-on-one conversations.

This is easily remedied: always repeat the question! Whether or not there are audience microphones available, I repeat *any* question asked. Most importantly, this allows everyone to hear the question. And because you're repeating or restating it, the question asker can clarify, if needed, and you can respond or ask further questions.

Another strategy I use is to walk around the room during my talk. This helps people feel I am talking directly to them, and I can sense when they may have additional questions. Bonus: it calms any jitters, either on their part or mine. Success all the way around!

— CHAPTER 7 EXERCISE —

This exercise is a two-parter that will help you become more confident and stay that way, both at the beginning of your talk and as you wind up.

For your beginning: Pull out your CV or bio. If it's longer than a short paragraph, now's the time to adjust it. Try rewriting it using a maximum of five sentences. What do you want people to know most? Think of the old journalistic five Ws and an H: who, what, when, where, why, and how.

For your windup: Ask a colleague or friend to listen to part of your talk, or if you're pressed for time, demonstrate a short summary for them. Next, have them ask you three to five questions about what you've covered. Don't peek—let their questions be new for you. Your goal is to (a) answer the questions, being sure to repeat them, and (b) ask for their feedback on what you accomplished.

CHAPTER 8
THE ART OF REHEARSAL:
PRACTICE MAKES PERFECT (ALMOST)

CLOSE YOUR EYES AND IMAGINE THE BEST, MOST ENGAGING play or movie you've seen. If you're like me, you've noticed that we don't always get a glimpse of what goes on behind the scenes. We don't see how the actors rehearse their lines, or the stage manager marks positions on set, or the costumer creates a costume that perfectly suits the characters.

We also may not realize what it actually takes to ensure a production (a play, a movie, our presentation) is seamless, smooth, and polished. It takes a lot of effort to be effortless! When it comes to rehearsing for a presentation, I like to take my cues right from the stage.

Just as acting is all about finding the balance between spontaneity and the script, so is speaking in public or even leading a meeting. Actor Stacy Keach explained it this way: "In rehearsal you should research as many alternate ways as possible to express yourself. The more choices you have at your disposal the better your performance will be, because you can be spontaneous and the other actor will respond spontaneously."

When you're preparing for a presentation, you can absolutely try different ways to convey your message and influence your intended audience, exactly the way you want to. And even though you're likely not waiting for another actor onstage, you still want to prime the path for a conversation with your own audience. Your "audience" could be your boss, your peers, your team, the C-suite, or even a large group.

Often we procrastinate when it comes to rehearsing a conversation or presentation. We think it will take too much time. Or we're timid about seeing ourselves on camera or hearing our voice on a recording (who isn't!). Perhaps we're reluctant to practice in front of a colleague. Maybe we just have too many other duties that take priority.

Not long ago, I was working on a leadership presentation for a client on this very topic: how to be more influential by improving your presentation skills. I sent out a short survey to this senior-level group.

One of the key questions was "How do you rehearse?" Of course, I included space for comments, and they filled it up! Interestingly, over 60 percent stated that they "wing it," meaning they tend not to rehearse at all or procrastinate so long they have to make it up on the fly.

While there is definitely something to be said for versatility and spontaneity, I guarantee you that great athletes and actors alike really do prepare in advance. They want to take advantage of every possible edge to come out on top, and so do you. When I work with clients in workshops or one-on-one and small group coaching, we spend a lot of time on how to rehearse.

Sometimes, the toughest part is just beginning! When I queried these senior leaders on why they chose not to rehearse, some simply said, "I don't know how to start."

Surprisingly, this happens to even the best or most famous people. In an interview with actor Cate Blanchett on the show *60 Minutes*, reporter Lesley Stahl asked her about her work and how she prepares. Ms. Blanchett's reply: "The trickiest thing is beginning. It's kind of tricking yourself; the confidence trick. Like an athlete does, you have to just say: 'I'm just going to start. I'm ready. I'm open. Let's go.'"

So, let's rock! Here's how you can take advantage of the art of rehearsal, right back in your own office. The good news is, you may already be doing this without even realizing it!

HAVE A BACKUP PLAN

I'm a girl with a plan, and I like—and use—the concept of having a Plan A, a Plan B, and even a Plan C, because stuff happens. Perhaps you're getting ready to lead an important meeting with a counterpart. You're handling the people part and she's handling the technical part, only you've just gotten word that she will be late. Or, you're on a panel at an industry conference, and people seem to be walking in and out, "sampling" a few sessions. Or, worse yet, the power goes out. What will you do?

A few years ago, a U.S. colleague and I were invited to work with a group of upcoming real estate trainers for some classes in India. We were very excited about delivering this training. Our task was both to train them on our material and to ensure their teaching and facilitation skills were excellent.

The training included all aspects of commercial, retail, and multifamily real estate, and we had to cover a series of courses over a week's period. Despite our own team's research and client conversations, we weren't sure how experienced this team actually was, so we devised a few ways to simultaneously help them learn the material and learn how to teach it themselves. This was essential since they would be facilitating classes on it in the future. To ensure we covered everything, our initial plans were to teach a summary of each of the four all-day courses on our itinerary. As they say, the best-laid plans often go awry!

Ten minutes into our first day, I realized that our original plan wasn't going to work. Plans A, B, and C weren't going to work. Although this team was very smart and fully engaged, this material on all things commercial real estate was completely new to them, as was the brand-new real estate market in our location. I had a quick flash of pure panic and broke out in a cold sweat! I remember thinking, *Oh my goodness. How is this going to work?*

Because I knew the material upside down, inside out, and sideways, I was able to pivot right away, and this proved to be crucial to our success. I knew we couldn't possibly pack every single nugget in, so I decided to layer it. I started with the most important parts of each course, then included those in the next level of importance, and so on, gauging my audience's participation, reactions, and questions throughout. All was going well, *until . . .*

The power went out! We were in an older office building with few windows, so it was completely dark and pretty warm. A porter arrived with candles, water, ice, and Coca-Colas, and we kept on going. I had been using my Mac laptop, and my colleague had brought her iPad (part of that Plan B!), so we gathered the students around both devices to see the course material.

Soon, it became unbearably hot and steamy in this small room, and there was still no power. I could tell our students were uncomfortable (and so was I). Time for Plan C!

I decided to take the class outside. After all, we were discussing real estate, so why not get the whole team out of a hot, dark room and into the outdoors? We went on a short, previously unplanned property tour and continued our discussions. It actually worked really well—it was a new experience, it allowed participants to see how to apply what we'd been discussing, and we had the opportunity to chat with each other. Success! This approach could have worked for just about any topic.

Now, that situation may not happen to all of us, but there is an almost 100 percent chance that something else will, so it pays to be prepared. It's truly the art of rehearsal: being so conversant and composed in your material knowing your material so well that you can pivot in any direction and still stay on track. The key is to decide in advance how you could handle different scenarios.

EDIT FIRST

You've written down all your notes for an upcoming presentation or important conversation, and you think you're ready to rehearse. Well, maybe. This scenario may sound familiar:

I was chatting with a colleague about an important presentation he was about to make to his leadership team. He looked a little worried, so I asked what was bothering him most and how I could help.

Immediately, he replied, "I can't put my finger on it. I think I'm including too much stuff. And I don't know where to look. I'm just feeling scattered."

This happens to the best of us. Often we want to include *all* the information we have, usually for several reasons: we want to display our knowledge, we feel it builds our credibility, or it just makes us feel comfortable. The secret here is editing, editing, editing. You have to become a ruthless editor.

When I work with my clients, we spend a lot of time on this. Why? Because it can take some time to get it right. In my small group and one-on-one workshops, I ask participants to show me an outline of their talk or conversation. Almost always, they like to script it out, and they often return to me with pages and pages of notes. And almost always, they are reluctant to give up what they've already written.

If this sounds familiar, don't worry! I'll give you a few of the top tactics I use with my clients to solve this. To be influential, you'll often have to strike a delicate balance between not including absolutely everything and providing enough context to allow someone to make a decision or take action.

Hit Your Top Three
When you feel you're almost ready to rehearse, edit first.

Review the three main ideas you plan to convey, and be sure you're carrying those thoughts throughout your presentation. This is a good time to take a quick look again at the Power of Three in Chapter 4. I always do this, no matter how long my presentation is. This works because when you rehearse, what you've written down previously on slides or paper may sound different when it comes out of your mouth!

Try this: Start your rehearsal by thinking of your presentation as an elevator pitch. Whether or not it actually is one doesn't matter. What matters is that you can state what your talk is about in a maximum of thirty seconds. When I practice this with my clients, I ask them to state their message in twenty words or less. I recommend trying this in front of someone who doesn't know your topic. If they can easily understand what you're trying to convey, so will others. If they can't, it's time to go back to the drawing board!

Connect Those Dots
How you choose to weave in relevant stories and examples may actually have more impact than data in some cases. It's important to remember that a pile of stories is exactly that—just a pile. Make sure you tie in each story or example you tell throughout your presentation. I keep a list of the examples and stories I plan to use and cross-check them to be sure I've done exactly that.

Try this: Revamp your notes. If your notes are too lengthy, you will either end up reading them or find yourself frantically thumbing through them, looking for what you want to say. Start with the expectation that you'll cull your notes down.

You can do this by using a highlighter to spotlight your major points. Or you can simply list bullet points. When you do this, you'll be able to focus more on your presentation, rather than scrambling through your notes.

Try this: Say it out loud. You'd be surprised how many of us speed through our rehearsals, perhaps just reading our notes while sitting at our desks. This doesn't work! I confess, I've relayed many a thought or presentation idea to my golden retriever. His reaction is always positive and enthusiastic—that's great, but a little more audience feedback is helpful.

Try this: Stand up, then look up, both when you rehearse and when you're in your final presentation. I find this technique very effective and use it every time; you can use it too. Even if you may be sitting at a conference table or dialing into a virtual conference from your desk for your presentation, stand up when you practice.

Here's why: Standing automatically makes your posture different. It makes your voice sound different too.

Then, look up. We want to see your face, not the top of your head, when you're talking. This is especially important in a virtual presentation, as we sometimes want to look down at our notes, giving our audience a great view of our heads and not the rest of us.

Try this: As you're rehearsing, keep your intended impact in mind. Your audience wants to feel confident in your knowledge, and they want to learn from you. Equally important, they want to understand the impact of what you're saying: how it will affect them. This is particularly crucial when you're presenting to the C-suite. Make sure you understand how you will convey what the issue is, why they should care about it, and, finally, how you recommend or plan to solve the problem.

Try this: Do a self-video. Yes, you've got it! Nearly everyone today has a cell phone with a great camera, and we're used to taking selfies. Self-videos are an excellent way to see how you actually come across "onstage," especially when the pressure hits. You'll be able to hear how you sound and whether you're using too many filler words such as "um," "ah," or "like." You will also notice if you're fidgeting and whether you appear confident and conversational.

I recommend using this tactic right after you finish writing your presentation. Don't wait. Not only can you see how you appear, but you can instantly tell if what you plan to say is showing up as you intended. It's also useful to let this first video marinate a little in your head. Be sure to write down notes on what you loved and what you feel you could do even better. For more tips on best practices for self-videos, review the exercises in Chapters 3 and 6.

HOW MANY TIMES SHOULD I REHEARSE?

If you're like most of my clients and colleagues, you want to know how many times you should rehearse. One colleague whose initial notes were pretty lengthy recounted how she practiced every day for a presentation that was two weeks out. "It didn't work so well," she said. "I kept changing things, and it turned out to be more confusing than it was in the first place!"

It's true, you actually can practice too much. You don't want to cram like you did for an exam in high school or college. It's also true that there's no magic solution to this, but here's what has worked for me.

My rule of thumb is to practice three times. That's it. Ideally, I practice in front of someone. This could be in front of a colleague or even a friend. While you may not have an entire audience in front of you, you do have a live person who can give you immediate feedback on how you look and sound, and on whether your delivery comes off well. At minimum, rehearse in front of a mirror so you can see yourself.

Whatever way you choose, always try to mimic what it will look like in real life; you can do this, for example, by wearing the same outfit you plan to wear for your presentation.

Here's my sequence for how I rehearse:

1. I rehearse the first time right after I finish writing and preparing the presentation. This is to see and hear whether what's coming out of my mouth matches what I intended when I wrote it.
2. I practice a second time after I make any adjustments needed. For instance, perhaps I've included a story or example that doesn't flow well or doesn't fit at all. I can tweak it or perhaps even save it for another presentation.
3. Finally, about five to seven days before my event, I do a final rehearsal, just to make sure all is in place as I like it. I definitely take advantage of any opportunity to check out the room where I'll be presenting, but I don't typically rehearse there.

CHECK YOUR LOGISTICS: SIX TIPS FOR SUCCESS

Now that you've practiced what you're going to say and how you'll deliver it, it's important to check your logistics. This may not break your presentation, but with technology changing ever so quickly, it can certainly stall it. You never know what can happen.

When I first began teaching overseas, I had to use a client-produced version of translated slides, and their organizer was to provide me with a USB drive when I arrived at the venue. You know how you can tell when something is going to go sideways? Well, it happened that day! A few hours before we were to begin, I asked for the USB and was told it was "coming soon." After asking repeatedly, I started to feel a bit sick to my stomach! What would I do if it didn't arrive? When pressed, my contact finally showed up with a USB, handed it to me, and said, "This is it, madam!" Not so much. I popped it into my Mac, and . . . it was local folk songs! Suffice it to say, this wasn't going to work. Fortunately, I'm persistent, and we were able to get the correct material, although it did take a little extra work. To ensure a successful presentation, here are six questions to ask about logistics:

1 Whose Computer Will You Use?

I always ask my client or the organizer or association what the tech requirements are. Don't assume it will be fine; ask for confirmation. This is important if you will have slides, photos, polls, or anything else to display on-screen. For example, will you be using your own laptop or someone else's? I prefer to use my own Mac if at all possible. It allows me better control, for one thing. Additionally, if I am using slides, the fonts and colors may shift on someone else's computer, especially if it isn't Mac friendly or there's a firewall.

2 What Capabilities Do You Require?

I often need wireless or sound, as I like to have walk-in music and may play a video or use a polling app. Always, always test this in advance, and then have a Plan B, anyway! My Plan B is to go low tech if the high tech doesn't work for some reason, and I tell the audience exactly that. I confess I like my walk-in music loud, so it helps to test the volume, too, so you can adjust it if needed as your room fills up.

Even if I'm using an organizer's internal polling function, I always include a quick follow-up slide with the same poll question or answer, depending on what I'm talking about. That way, whether or not the polling function works, we're golden, and I can just talk about the results or ask another question.

3 What Other Equipment or Setup Do You Need?

This can depend on where you're presenting. I always bring an extension cord, just in case, because laptop cords never seem long enough. This is especially true if I'll be presenting in a tighter conference room where it's easy to trip over a cord. If I'm going to be in a hotel or conference center, they'll likely have any needed cords, but because I have a Mac, I always bring my own adapter or two. I've been known to leave them at a venue!

I ask for a mic in advance if it looks like it will be needed. For me, this is usually if the audience is over about fifty people, but that may differ depending on the size and configuration of the room. For example, if you find out you'll be in a ballroom but the audience will be small, you may want to secure a mic so your voice doesn't get lost. Be sure to ask for audience microphones if you'll need them for any questions.

4 Where's the remote?

I like to bring my own. My current favorite is an easy-to-use Logitech remote that charges via USB, but if you prefer to use your host's remote, just confirm in advance.

5 Did You Bring a Clock?

It's important to be on time, and not all rooms have a clock, so I bring my own. I prefer not to have to look at my phone for the time if I don't have to, but you can use a digital clock or timer. I use a simple analog clock from the drugstore. Sometimes, less is more.

6 Where Will You Put Your Stuff?

I don't use a podium or a head table unless it's required. Because I primarily do workshops, I prefer to be down on the floor with my audience, although I am sometimes in a ballroom on a stage.

Either way, I ask for a small table to put my laptop on so I can see it. It's also convenient if you need to have any handouts at the ready. This way, I can see my slides if needed without having to turn upstage to view them on screen. If there's a confidence monitor on the front of the stage facing me, this is not needed.

WHAT IF IT'S HYBRID?

I had the experience of doing what I call a super-hybrid presentation, and it was like no other—the logistics alone were tremendous. This was for a class that was being conducted in Asia; the participants were on the ground there, and I was seven thousand miles away, in my home office. The issues were interesting, to be sure.

The venue was a new one for this client. With about thirty-five participants seated classroom style (with tables), there were several huge columns in the way. Although I was on the jumbotron (aka Zoom screen), those columns made it tough to see both the participants and the other instructors I was working with.

What made it even more interesting was that this was a translated class. If I were there in person, I'd have a translator following me, first translating what I said, then relaying responses and questions from the room. Since that wasn't possible, I had two simultaneous translators (thank goodness!), one in each ear. It was a lot to listen to, and we had to adapt both on the fly and in another language, but it worked. Each evening after the session, we all met to discuss how it went and cover any questions, whether with the content or the translation.

Now, you may not have to do this kind of super-hybrid presentation, but if you're doing any type of virtual or hybrid presentation, it pays to check it out first. You'll need to know how the system will work, how the virtual participants will hear you and each other, and how any group activities will work. And, of course, you'll want to follow each of my six steps for hybrid success. The same concepts apply, and this is definitely repeatable!

— CHAPTER 8 EXERCISE —

Try this two-part exercise in your own office or at home.

Solidify your pregame routine: When you finish reading this chapter, make a list of ten things you currently do on the day of your presentation. This could include anything from having only one cup of coffee to checking your outfit to grabbing your notes, or actually writing even more notes.

Next, write down five things you don't do yet but would like to incorporate, and then describe how you'll do them for your next presentation. Keep this on hand. Soon, you'll have a pregame checklist, and it will become a habit to use it each and every time you present.

CHAPTER 9
WHEN QUESTIONS FLY!
HANDLING QUESTIONS SUCCESSFULLY

I'M A LITTLE WORRIED ABOUT HANDLING POTENTIAL QUESTIONS. What if I don't know the answer? Does this sound familiar? I can relate, and I bet you can too. When I consult or do executive coaching, how to confidently answer questions is always at the top of everyone's list.

When questions fly and we *aren't* prepared, we wind up feeling rattled and our presentation can quickly go sideways. This especially comes into play when you're presenting to executive leadership or leading a high-stakes meeting, or even when you're copresenting and not sure what the other person is going to say.

A few years ago, I was invited to moderate a panel for a large industry event. We had three or four expert panelists, plus me, and a packed house.

We did our homework in advance (or so I thought) and had several meetings via phone to cover our topic and who could best address each area. I was asked to be at a podium, and our panelists were seated next to me. After we were graciously introduced by our host, I asked the first question of our first panelist. All right, I remember thinking, *here we go!*

But instead of answering the question as we'd rehearsed, he immediately let out a rant against the association we were presenting for. He had an issue with the organization ignoring one of his requests and was essentially venting about it. Loudly. You could have heard a pin drop; the audience was pretty much surprised into silence. Yikes!

You can guess what my reaction was—this really gave me cause for pause!

What did I do? Although I admit I very much wanted to pull him right off the stage, of course I did not. I managed to compose myself quickly and took the simplest route: I thanked him for sharing his opinion, told him we could discuss it offline, and moved right on to the next panelist and the next question. You could definitely see everyone's shoulders relax!

The truth is, unusual things happen no matter how well we plan. Sometimes even the most well-intended questions or comments can derail our train of thought and our conversation or presentation. Often people will ask or want to talk about anything, even if it's unrelated to the topic at hand. Or maybe we're not as prepared as we hoped.

We want to guide the energy in the room and keep everything moving forward. If it's our meeting or talk, this makes things easier. But sometimes it isn't. Either way, here are a few examples of how questions can easily throw you off track. You may recognize them:

- You're hoping people will ask questions at the end, but they start interjecting.
- One person has a louder voice (literally or figuratively) and just keeps on talking.
- Someone else professes to be an expert on the topic you're discussing.
- There's a distraction in the room or the nearby hallway.
- You haven't exactly planned how to address questions.
- You're running out of time.
- No one asks anything.

If you're like me, you've experienced some or all of these situations.

Imagine this: you're almost at the end of your talk or meeting, and you're feeling relieved. Then you realize a few people are starting to rustle in their seats. Some of them are even looking at their phones or talking with each other. And you're running a little late, which is making you feel rattled. This is partly because you encountered an unexpected tech glitch in the middle of your presentation and decided to let everyone take a quick restroom break while you fixed it.

It took a longer than expected to fix the issue, and now the flow of your session has been interrupted. Unfortunately, you forgot to let people know when to return, and they are still straggling in. You take a quick glance at the audience and notice there are a few more vacant seats than there were earlier.

Gulp! Now you're feeling even more awkward. You aren't exactly sure how to wind up your session, so you brightly ask if anyone has questions. Your request lands with a resounding *thunk!*

No one says anything. You quickly thank everyone for coming and end your talk.

Is this memorable? Not in the best way. But it is common; almost everyone has experienced something similar. I was sitting in on a virtual presentation recently where the opposite occurred. The participants had lots of questions. It was moving along well until one attendee wanted to zero in on a situation particular to her own business. The host didn't want to offend this attendee by cutting her off, so she let her keep talking . . . and talking.

The result was that no one else had a chance to ask questions, and guess what? They tuned out and began dropping off the call.

When this happens, it's just like a tumbleweed gathering speed in a windstorm. It goes faster and faster, and you can lose both control of the situation and the opportunity to effectively get your message across. Sometimes, when something breaks our concentration or our focus is diverted, we stumble and our presentation derails or goes off track.

Losing control of an awkward situation can make you even more nervous. Can you get the conversation back in your court? Absolutely! At minimum, how we handle questions and distractions that arise demonstrates our versatility and flexibility as a presenter. At best, our ability to guide our audience to where we want them to be enhances our credibility. It's a key ingredient to a successful presentation!

Here's how to do it. First, think about what you can do in advance:

PUT YOUR PEDAL TO THE METAL

This is a great time to put your pedal to the metal and think about how you've been preparing for your presentation. Don't underestimate the value of DYH—Doing Your Homework. When you're prepared, you'll feel comfortable and poised, and not only will your delivery be smooth, you'll be ready for questions, too!

Try this: I always remember my boss's voice saying, "What have you found out? Do your homework!" When I do presentation skills coaching with my clients, I tell them that as they prepare for their own next best presentation, I want them to hear my voice saying the same exact thing. I want you to hear this too—I promise, it really works.

WRITE IT DOWN

When you're getting ready for a presentation, it pays to write down your thoughts and ideas in advance. I recommend you write down questions too. Yes, it's often easier to add notes to your phone or computer, but I find that those ideas are stickier when I actually put pencil to paper, or marker to whiteboard. And here's the good news: this does double duty!

If you want to turn your presentation from ordinary to extraordinary, use a whiteboard or a flip chart to "park" questions you either don't know the answer to or want to defer. This is a really good way to make sure information you promise to participants isn't forgotten when the session is over. I have a rolling whiteboard with a simple Post-it flip chart attachment (the best inexpensive hack ever).

Try this: As you're working on the structure of your presentation and adding your ideas, add questions too. I recommend jotting down two types of questions.

- **Questions and ideas you might want to use to round out your talk:**
  - How else do you think you could use this information when you're back in your office or at home?
  - How can you reinforce your message so people will remember it?

Note that I've used the word *ideas*; this is purposeful. Scripting out your ideas will help you find the context, or what I call the "flavor," of your talk. This *doesn't* mean, however, that you have to actually voice all of them!

It's important to remember that the questions you ask will depend on the situation. For example, if I'm meeting with my CEO, I probably won't actually *ask* them, "What will make the difference in my presentation?" This is something they will expect me to already know! *But*, it's key for me to do my homework and think of it "behind the scenes." This means I'm answering their questions and helping to solve their problems during our conversation or presentation.

■ **Questions you feel people will (or could) ask:**
Anticipating what people want to know is a huge help. I'll often ask friends or colleagues in advance what they would want to know or what kinds of questions they have.

For example, if I'm leading a workshop on how to manage challenging conversations, I'll ask a small group of connections what trips them up or what solutions they have tried. I was chatting with a fashion stylist about being on her podcast, and we were discussing current trends in office wear for both men and women. We decided that before the podcast, I would take a quick poll to ask friends and colleagues how they dress in their offices.

People are typically happy to help. This also lets me know if I'm on track with my content and gives me intel on what questions could come up.

When you've come up with your questions, you can easily list these off to the side of your whiteboard or paper; I make it easy on myself by marking an outline around them so they stand out.

HAVE THE MEETING BEHIND THE MEETING

Jack, a young professional I know, ran to catch up with me after a meeting. "How can I be more relatable?" he asked. "I feel I'm friendly, but I always get stuck in the introductions, and I'm not sure what to do." Here's the key: start *before* your meeting. It's all about how you weave those communications together before you even begin.

You can use this technique whether you're doing a pitch or presentation or leading a meeting with several departments. I call it "the meeting behind the meeting." If you're a natural networker, you may already be doing this. It's easier when you feel like you're part of the audience and not at the front of the room!

Perhaps you're working on an idea or project that is cross-departmental or requires other leaders' buy-in. This can be challenging to do during a meeting—you never know what surprises will occur.

The best way I've found to do this is to work on getting some intel in advance. Ideally, you want to chat in advance with those leaders who will make a decision, be impacted by that decision, or move a project forward. Find out what they think about it first, what questions they have, and how they rate the idea or project's chance of success.

You may not find out everything you'll want to know, but chances are, you can find out something! What you will hear is what they're thinking, what's top of mind, and what their expectations are.

HAVE A PLAN A FOR ANSWERING QUESTIONS

This is actually a two-parter, because your Plan B will be in real time. Decide in advance what framework you'd like to use for questions that may arise. Do you want to take questions during your talk or have a Q&A at the end? There's no right answer to this. In either scenario, you'll want to maintain control of the questions so you don't get off track.

Again, the simplest way to do this involves anticipation. A colleague chatted with me after a recent presentation, asking for some advice. "I thought it was going well," he said, "until I realized I hadn't thought about this in advance."

One way to head this off is to use a pack of good old-fashioned index cards. You can put them on tables or chairs and ask people to list a question and pass them up to the front. I recommend asking someone ahead of time to collect them for you; that way, you'll feel more prepared. Think about what you can do in real time:

WORK THE ROOM

I love to "work the room," and here are my simple tricks for doing it successfully.

Arrive early. There are several reasons to do this, which we discussed in Chapter 3. The main reason I like to arrive early is so I can meet and greet people. I can introduce myself to participants, welcome them in, and thank them for coming.

Not only that, I can ask them what they are hoping to learn or find out in my session. This immediately makes them feel even more invested in the workshop or session, because we have met each other and they feel welcome. When they tell me what they are hoping to hear, that's gold! It provides instantaneous intel. I can then decide whether to use the feedback or not, or how I want to work it in. What could be better?

I may go one step further and ask, "Mary, you just made a great point about how we can communicate better. I'm wondering, if I bring that up during our session, would it be okay if I ask you to add your thoughts or mention your comment?"

Most people will say yes. If they aren't comfortable with it or are shy about speaking up, I just smile and say okay. Either way, I gain buy-in—they almost immediately sense that I'm approachable and inviting them into the conversation. And I can always ask another participant.

Say I've asked Mary and she's agreed to add a comment when this topic comes up, but she freezes or is suddenly shy. The same principle works here: I thank her and offer the opportunity to another audience member.

WHEN SOMEONE MAKES A STATEMENT

What if you ask for questions and someone steps up to the audience microphone and merely makes a statement? For example: "I think people today don't communicate as well as they used to." When I consult with clients, they're often stumped by this; they don't know what to do and don't want to offend the participant.

The answer to this is often simple. It's okay to ask the participant, "Can you please clarify your question?" or even better, "Are you asking about *(fill in the blank)*"? If you don't understand the question, there's a good chance your audience won't either.

GET READY TO IMPLEMENT: HAVE A PLAN B

Always, always have a Plan B (and a Plan C). Trust me, you'll thank me later! One more tip I like to use is to write down a few preplanned questions in advance. This accomplishes a few things: If no one brings up any questions, I have a few at the ready. Better yet, I've written them down, just in case I forget. And best of all, I look poised and comfortable. This is definitely a winner!

If you're prepared, you'll know the structure and flow of your talk or conversation in advance, you'll have a Plan B in your pocket in case anything changes or goes awry, and most importantly, you will feel natural and at ease, no matter what questions come up.

Handling questions successfully is often a worry point for many of us. You might call it a fear of the unknown! We're concerned that we won't know an answer, we'll be put on the spot, or we won't look as cool, calm, and collected as we'd like to.

It does take practice. It's helpful to try the tips and tactics in this chapter *before* that high-stakes conversation or presentation lands in your lap.

If you can practice these with a colleague or friend or even in a lower-stakes meeting, you'll feel more comfortable simply because you got out there and did it!

— CHAPTER 9 EXERCISE —

Pull up an upcoming presentation you're working on or even a past one. For each section of the presentation, write down three questions that participants already asked (if you've done the presentation), or that you feel they may ask (if it's a new presentation).

Doing this exercise helps you anticipate questions that may come up, which areas may require more explanation, and where examples or stories can work to your advantage. As we discussed in earlier chapters, you may not wind up using all of the questions you write down, and that's okay!

CHAPTER 10
BODY LANGUAGE:
WHAT ARE YOU NOT SAYING?

RECENTLY, A COLLEAGUE WAS PREPARING FOR HER FIRST presentation in front of a leadership group. She called me to ask how to elevate the way she carries herself when she walks into a room. "I'm worried that my body language won't match what I say," she said. This is what happened during her presentation:

My colleague began to notice that her audience seemed to be drifting away. Some were scrolling on their phones or talking with each other. A few brought out their laptops. And a few even left the room.

What was the issue? I asked her how she felt up in front of the group. Did she feel nervous? Was she able to get buy-in from her audience?

Rooted in one spot at the front of the room with her arms crossed, my colleague couldn't see her slides and had to turn to face the screen when she spoke. Did they tune her out? You bet. She didn't stand a chance with this leadership audience.

Here's why: Your nonverbal communication—your body language—and your voice speak for you. They often carry even more weight than your message itself. Think about it: body language encompasses nonverbal behavior such as eye contact, facial expressions, posture, and gestures. When your body language gets in the way of what you're saying, or your voice lacks variety, volume, and pitch, it can turn any audience off.

In any conversation or presentation, the key to influencing others is not just what we say but how we say it and how we present ourselves, even before we walk into the room.

I learned an early lesson in this. When I was twelve years old, I was tall for my age, and my mom was determined that I shouldn't try to hide it. Her solution: I had to practice walking around the house with a book on my head, which she felt would improve my posture.

There was an upside to spending all that time with a book on top of my head, literally. Now, I'm 5'9" and I don't slump!

BEYOND WORDS

Our nonverbal communication can absolutely enhance and punctuate what we say, or it can be disastrous. Have you ever had a conversation with someone whose smile didn't match their eyes? Then you know what I mean.

This is especially true when we're leading a meeting, making a pitch, or doing a presentation. For example, a client asked me to coach one of her leaders and to specifically take notice of her behavior in meetings. "I'm not sure if it's just that she is feeling casual or what," my client relayed, "but this leader is too transparent. If she doesn't like something that's said in a meeting or she disagrees with it, she will actually roll her eyes, and it happens more than once!"

When I worked with this leader, I discovered that she wasn't tuned in to the fact that her emotions were displayed right on her face. A small habit had become a bigger, and unwelcome, habit. What was the solution? We worked with her to alleviate this nonverbal communication issue—it was something she had to focus on and remind herself of prior to each meeting, especially when she knew her opinions could differ.

It's almost as if our brains are working overtime! Psychologist and facial recognition expert Dr. Paul Ekman studied cross-cultural body language. You may have heard of Dr. Ekman; his research was the basis for the TV show *Lie to Me*. He identified two main types of universal expressions: macro expressions and micro expressions.

Macro expressions are our normal facial expressions and typically match the context and tone of what we say. For instance, if you're congratulating a coworker on a promotion, you may greet them with a big smile that goes from your mouth all the way to the little crinkles in the corner of your eyes. That's a macro expression.

On the other hand, let's say you really wanted that promotion and feel your colleague is not as deserving as you. You walk up to that colleague to offer congratulations, but your smile is tight and your eye contact is neutral. That is a micro expression.

YOUR BODY LANGUAGE SPEAKS FOR YOU

Both types of expressions play a huge part in any conversation or presentation. This is because often people can easily tell when something is amiss or someone is "faking it," but they may not know exactly why. Ekman says our emotions show up regularly on our faces, whether we like it or not. When you're planning a presentation, it pays to consider what your body language conveys, especially when it conflicts with what you say.

Macro expressions are often what we notice first. They can last anywhere from a half second to four seconds, according to Ekman. They are often a demonstration of happiness or excitement. However, these macro expressions can also show emotions like sadness or anger. This can include an open posture—think palms open and up—and well-timed hand gestures.

Pay attention to this when you rehearse. It's helpful to see how you appear in your self-video. Write down each of the gestures you used and when they happened within the context of your presentation. Then you can go back and edit those gestures accordingly. For example, I use my hands a lot when I'm talking. I check this in my own self-videos, and I also use a prop: a water bottle. Of course, this helps if I am thirsty, but I use it mainly because it gives me something to hold and anchors my hand. You can try this, too, with a water bottle or a small pad of paper.

Micro expressions are those involuntary emotions that show up on our faces. They tend to appear almost instantly and are short in duration: a half second or less. These micro expressions show what we're truly feeling, despite what we're saying: disgust, fear, or surprise, for example. And if you are someone who wears your heart on your sleeve, we'll know it!

When I work with companies and associations to improve their communication and communication skills, we spend time focusing on body language and voice, and we almost always do a video.

In my workshops, I like to do an activity called "Read the Room." This is a really effective and fun activity that teaches participants the impact their body language and voice have on their conversations and presentations. Participants break into small groups and speak to each other one by one on any topic they like, personal or professional. The kicker is that they must talk in gibberish! The goal is for each group to see if they can understand what the speaker is talking about, mostly through body language and tone of voice. When the activity is done, participants always relay that it is an eye-opening experience!

BODY LANGUAGE DOs AND DON'Ts

The next time you present, remember these pointers to increase your own awareness:

DO:

- Stand still or move purposefully.
- Always face your audience.
- Maintain eye contact—find a few friends in the audience.
- Take those hands out of your pockets—use open, face-up palms.
- Keep your facial expression open.

DON'T:

- Fidget with your hair, clothes, or props (e.g., a pen, notes).
- Sway from side to side.
- Turn your back on the audience.
- Look into space.
- Put your hands in your pockets.
- Scrunch up your face.

Use These Tactics to Improve Your Nonverbal Communication

The next time you're preparing for a presentation, try these tactics:

■ Know When to Move

If you've ever watched a presenter or leader pace back and forth over and over again, you know what you'll remember from that performance is exactly that—the pacing. To get your listeners to focus on what you're saying, I like to turn to the theater for some valuable tips on when to move.

The next time you watch a play or a movie, notice that the actors' movements are carefully choreographed. This is called blocking; each and every movement has a purpose. When actors rehearse a scene, they are not only practicing their lines, they are also practicing their movements so they enhance, not detract from, their words.

■ **Script It Out**

Even if you're not an actor, you, too, can script out your talk to get you going. This doesn't always work well if you're on the fly, but it does work when you can jot down a few notes ahead of time. I like to move around the room during a presentation, and I always like to scan the room in advance so I can see what my options are.

For example, are the tables placed far enough apart that I can move between them? Will anything be blocking my audience's view of me (or mine of theirs) while I'm speaking, such as a column? Is there a door to a corridor behind me where luncheon servers are going in and out?

■ **Move the Audience**

Just as you script out your own movements, script out movements for your audience. I plan in advance whether I'm going to have them stand for an activity, take a stretch break, or break out into smaller groups. When you choose to do this depends on whether you're trying to punctuate a point, encourage more people to talk in smaller groups, or simply take a break.

Depending on the length of your talk, these tactics can also be useful if you need to change direction or if there is a disruption you need to quell. You will also need to consider where you're presenting and who your audience is. Note that these techniques may work differently in other countries where the sense of personal space may differ.

Tips for Using Your Voice Effectively

■ **Listen to Your Voice**

You may be familiar with an old FedEx commercial with John Moschitta at a business meeting talking faster, faster, and even faster.

Sometimes we are so anxious about our meeting, speech, or presentation that we talk at breakneck speed just to get through it! In fact, I was chatting with a client recently about her upcoming presentation, and we decided to have her rehearse on our virtual screen. Our objective was to see how she sounded, so I closed my eyes and just listened.

Here's what I heard: She was in a rush, there was no punctuation (it was almost one run-on paragraph), and her words were jumbled. I guess you could say she achieved her goal of getting through the presentation in a flash!

But here's the kicker: I didn't really understand what she said. Because she was speaking so quickly and didn't articulate well, I had a hard time just catching up with what she was saying. Your audience could feel the same way.

When I consult with clients on how to best boost their communication and presentation skills, we always spend some time on what their voice says about them.

■ **Control Your Pace**
The key here is to modulate both your voice and your delivery and force yourself not to hurry. This gives your audience time to absorb what you have just told them. If you tend to speed through your talk, write a simple reminder on a Post-it ("Go Slow!") and put your note where you can see it but the audience can't.

If you're delivering an important point or have information you want to emphasize, try pausing.

Yes, that's correct: take a pause! My clients often shudder when I say this, but it works. People don't mind if you take a quick pause; it allows them time to digest what you said and time for you to listen to their feedback or compose yourself, if needed. Conversely, if you want to heighten a dramatic story or example, pick up the pace a little and shorten your sentences or phrases.

Another way to pace yourself is to scan the audience lightly with your eyes. Not only are you making eye contact, you're almost automatically forcing yourself to slow down. You don't want to look like your eyes are continually going side to side, but this is easily corrected. Take in everyone at a glance first, and then return to those friendly faces for more direct eye contact.

Use your intuition here: you can use this tactic as a way to quickly pick out people who may be likely to answer any questions you pose later in your presentation.

■ **Vary Your Voice**
Whether you're meeting with a client, presenting on a panel or in a workshop, or doing a pitch, a monotone voice is a certain kiss of death! Showing a little variety with your voice will help keep your audience engaged throughout. There's also an unexpected side benefit: it will increase your own confidence *and* decrease your stage fright.

For example, practice changing the volume of your voice—up or down—to emphasize key points or emotions. Be sure to use some punctuation! A good way to practice this is to first review your notes. Whether you've scripted out your talk on paper or are using index cards or bullet points, underline or highlight where you can include more variety or pauses.

Remember, your audience will be observing your voice, your face, your hands, and your movements. The trick is to learn to use them to enhance, not distract from, your presentation. It just takes a little practice.

Here's my secret tactic; you can try it too, back in your own office.

— CHAPTER 10 EXERCISE —

It's all about how you arrive.

I love awards show season. When you watch an awards show—maybe the Oscars or the Grammys—perhaps you'll also see the celebrities arrive on the red carpet. I admit, I watch mostly to see what beautiful dresses, shoes, and outlandish outfits there are.

I also notice how the stars "arrive": how they walk, pose, smile, take a pause. Of course, many of these moments are curated, but you can use these same techniques.

First, when you walk into your next meeting, notice how you arrive.

Second, notice how others arrive and what their body language is. Who grabs your attention when they walk into a room? Observe, for example, who seems to naturally take the lead and who shrinks back. Or whose posture is open and friendly, and whose smile reaches their eyes.

And third, ask these four questions when you're giving your next presentation:

- Do you stop to say hello to people?
- Do you offer a smile or a handshake?
- Are people listening to you?
- Ask a colleague or friend to listen to your next talk. What are they hearing?

CHAPTER 11
CROSSING THE FINISH LINE

YOU LIKELY STARTED READING THIS BOOK BECAUSE YOU WERE wondering how to improve your communication and presentation skills. Perhaps you were getting ready to present a business case to your boss or your leadership team—the very next day. Or you were planning how to lead a meeting or be on your first panel. Maybe the opportunity to speak in public *sounded* great, but you didn't relish the idea of how on earth you could actually make it successful.

Sound familiar?

You might be facing the same obstacles many of my clients mention: feeling scattered or not knowing what to say, how to say it, or how to fit in everything you want to say. Or maybe just plain old fear!

Ninety-nine percent of the time (well, okay, 100 percent), overcoming these obstacles boils down to exactly three things: building confidence, preparing effectively, and editing what you say. Imagine you are constructing a building; what do you need first? The foundation. The same concept applies here. Confidence, preparation, and editing— these are the foundational items that will carry you through any presentation or conversation. Everything else stems from that.

Think of this book as helping you build your overarching umbrella of confidence, preparation, and editing. Implementing the advice in each section is what will get you to the finish line!

By now, you know that no matter what your role or field, or what your personal and professional goals, we all "sell"—we persuade others in some way, every day. We influence them to implement a plan, take action, and do what we need them to do. And we can achieve this most successfully by boosting how we communicate and present ourselves to others.

My goal has been to help you zero in on exactly that. You now have solid, surefire tactics and tips that you can use right away. Even if you don't pitch proposals every day, the skills you've learned in this book can absolutely help you paint the picture for your audience in any conversation or presentation.

Here's what we covered:

- Recognizing your fears about public speaking and discovering usable solutions
- Setting the foundation for any talk by first deciding on your topic using a SWOT analysis
- Determining the type of presentation you want
- Building confidence by discovering how to own the room and perfect your body language
- Learning to pivot in any conversation or presentation
- Recognizing the importance of having a Plan A, B, and even C
- Rehearsing effectively—a key element to success
- Hooking your audience and keeping them engaged
- Banishing the jitters!
- Taking the panic out of how to handle questions

Now, as mentioned at the beginning of this book, I want you to go back and look at the three areas you identified for yourself in the exercise from Chapter 1. As you answer the questions, think about not only the *what* but the *why*.

The next time you hear a speaker, any speaker, consider these questions. Write down how your responses may have changed or expanded as a result of everything you learned in this book.

- ▶ Did the presentation flow smoothly?
- ▶ Did the presenter seem relaxed and poised?
- ▶ Did the presenter have presence?
- ▶ Did the speaker's tone feel conversational?

- ▸ Was the presentation engaging?
- ▸ If the presenter used slides, did they add value?
- ▸ Was the overall setting pleasant?

Pull out the personal assessment you completed in the introductory chapter, but don't peek at your earlier responses. Instead, take it again. What areas have changed for you? Which ones came easily, and which were more challenging and may require more practice?

Throughout this book, I have included "doable" tips you can use to prepare and practice effectively. This includes the exercises at the end of each chapter, the "Try this" tips, videos, and one of my personal favorites: the whiteboard hack.

I hope you have enjoyed reading this book and working through the exercises as much as I have enjoyed creating them for you.

Now that you have all of these great tools at your disposal, go out and use them!

What's your next step? I can't wait to see you succeed!

I'd be delighted to chat with you personally about how we can work together on your communication and presentation skills success. I offer one-on-one and small group coaching, team workshops, and executive-level leadership meetings.

I invite you to visit my website, *LeadersExceed.com*, or contact me directly at *Shannon@LeadersExceed.com*.

 **Being a great presenter is easier than you think! You can do it!**

ACKNOWLEDGMENTS

I F YOU'VE EVER STEPPED FOOT ON A STAGE, LED A MEETING, OR had a conversation with your team, you know that it's the people behind the scenes who really make all the difference.

When I wrote my first book, *Say It With Success*, I didn't exactly have a process. I just wrote the book, found a copyeditor, and self-published it. The second one, *Strategies for Working with Small Tenants*, was published by an association that did all of the heavy lifting.

This time, I got smarter! I realized that writing a book—actually getting it out there—is exactly as hard as it sounds. I assembled a small "Be Influential" team that has indeed made all the difference in the success of this book and I am most grateful.

An enormous thank you goes to everyone on the *"Be Influential"* team who has helped me so much and enables me to do what I do. This includes my ever-fantastic virtual assistant team Gemma Baxter and Lizzie Giblin-Cook, LinkedIn expert Laura Taylor, PR guru Laura Perkes and stellar videographer Matt Bauer for showing up and for doing what they do best, every day.

To my exceptional editor, Nadia Geagea Pupa, and book management consultant Susie Schaefer, thank you. Nadia's expertise and creativity have helped me bring my ideas and stories to life in this book, even when they were well, a little crazy, and I wanted to brainstorm just one more time! Susie has patiently steered the path to making the finished book everything it can be, and more.

Although I'm the one writing the book, it has been my honor to learn from all of the individuals I have had the opportunity to lead or be led by, and to learn from you, my readers, thank you.

Finally, I want to thank my very special, ever-loving, ever-patient family, Jeff, Hayley, and Sarah. You are my motivation and my inspiration.

I'm delighted to have been able to work with and serve all of you. I'll see you next time!

Shannon Alter

ABOUT THE AUTHOR

Shannon Alter has a degree in theatre arts and is a Certified Property Manager (CPM®). She has leveraged her presentation skills and ability to communicate with anyone in the high-touch fields of real estate and hospitality. She speaks and trains leaders around the world and has written two books; she is a member of the Academy of Authors of the Institute of Real Estate Management (IREM), and wrote several recurring columns published in the *Journal of Property Management.*

Shannon lives in Southern California with her family, adores her Golden Retriever, and loves to travel just about anywhere. For more information, visit Shannon at *www.LeadersExceed.com.*

www.ingramcontent.com/pod-product-compliance
Lightning Source LLC
Chambersburg PA
CBHW020417130626
46549CB00006B/2600